ACTS OF TRUST

D1699691

ACTS OF TRUST

MAKING SENSE OF RISK, TRUST &
BETRAYAL IN OUR RELATIONSHIPS

MARY FARRELL
FOREWORD BY SUSAN WINTER

EXISLE
PUBLISHING

Dedicated to my father, Lionel Wise and my son, Joshua Farrell

First published 2005

Exisle Publishing Limited,
'Moonrising', Narone Creek Road, Wollombi, NSW 2325, Australia.
P.O. Box 60-490, Titirangi, Auckland 1230, New Zealand.
www.exislepublishing.com

Cataloguing-in-Publication Data
Farrell, Mary
Acts of trust : making sense of risk, trust and betrayal in our
relationships / by Mary Farrell.
Includes bibliographical references and index.
ISBN 0-908988-56-7
1. Trust. 2. Interpersonal relationships. I. Title.
158.2—dc 22

Text design and production by BookNZ
Cover design by Christabella Designs
Printed in China through Colorcraft Ltd, Hong Kong

Contents

Acknowledgements

I would like to thank my wonderful readers: Annette Asher, Eileen Birch, Guy Rubin and my husband Bill Farrell, for their patient and thorough reading of each chapter as this book progressed, and their unfailing and unflinching honesty. I could not have completed the book without them. I would also like to thank my transcriber, Tania Churches, whose accuracy and patience was invaluable.

Above all, I want to thank all my extraordinary subjects. All the people who appear in this book were immediately and enthusiastically responsive to my initial request to participate and there has seemed a particular synchronicity and purpose that has guided me to them. I feel deeply privileged to have shared their stories.

Thanks are due to the following for permission to reproduce copyright material:

Julie Matthews, for her song 'The Thorn upon the Rose', published by Circuit Music.

Macmillan Publishers, for the poem 'Victoria's Secret', from *Taking Off Emily Dickinson's Clothes* by Billy Collins.

Penguin Plays, for extracts from *Equus* by Peter Shaffer.

Vintage Publishers, for extracts from *Disgrace* by J.M. Coetzee.

Whurr Publishers, for an extract from *The Fragile Self* by Phil Mollon.

Foreword

My first introduction to Mary Farrell was via email. I was a contributing editor to a website that dealt with the emerging issues of modern female sexuality, empowerment, and intimate relationships. Her inquiry was related to a book I co-authored on older women and younger men. Having had two long-term committed relationships with much younger men, I found myself compelled to help other women navigate the known hurdles inherent in this type of cross-generational relationship. I was appreciative of yet another opportunity to speak out, clarify and express my thoughts and feelings on this widely misunderstood partnership. After I had learnt more about Mary's impressive background, and her desire to help others, we began our correspondence.

Mary sent pages of questions which I would answer in detail. Our conversations became progressively more open and revealing. Though she was writing from New Zealand, I sensed a human presence in the words she used and the languaging of her thoughts. The on-going process of interview was comfortable, despite the subject matter being intense. Her questions and subsequent responses were those of a brilliant academician. What intrigued and impressed me most was the unique combination of extreme intelligence tempered by great warmth.

I began to sense what it must be like to work with her professionally. She had the ability to draw out the essence of an experience, while creating an environment of trust. I felt free to expose the most intimate details of my life. I went back into my childhood, my mother's years of (then) active alcoholism and the emotional wedge it created between us. The violence, tension and chronic fear that dominated my youth was relived as we wandered through my childhood and adolescence, to get to the woman I am today. I saw Mary connecting the dots as she responded to my text. Each subsequent question was like that of an expert puzzle master, gently placing the pieces in order. She saw the big picture while extracting the details. As we continued our dialogue we delved into the deeper layers of the childhood experience. I had a profound love for my father, and he for me. It was natural and easy. We discussed at length how his love sustained me through my teenage years when my home life was at its worst.

Juxtaposed between these two individuals – my mother and my father – I received my initial template of love: what love looks like, how love expresses itself, and the nature of loving behaviour. I got the black and white … the polar opposites. But in between the contrasting edges of mother and father there was the whole picture, complete and yet perfect in its imperfection. It was my past, and my future.

Consciousness is an interesting process. I once heard a therapist say, 'Deal with it now, or deal with it later. But you will have to deal with it.' I have witnessed friends and associates who have run from themselves for a lifetime, as well as those who have embraced the process. Family of origin issues can trail us whether we understand them or not. But at some point in our lives we will have the choice, or the necessity, of shedding our outer mask. When the core of self wants to be acknowledged and seen and felt, it will prevail. Birth of any sort is a messy business, while at the same time a miracle.

Each year hundreds of new books appear, claiming to enlighten us, heal us, bring us inner peace or love, and even bridge the gender gap. As a population we are inundated with new techniques purporting to 'make it all make sense', teach us to gain inner wisdom, and even 'find our soulmate'. Yet the culminating result (for most of us) is that we are still struggling with issues of identity, intimacy and relationship. Evidently all the lectures, seminars, retreats, workshops and volumes of 'how to' books still don't lower the divorce rate or teach us how to stay in love. They can only give us breadcrumbs. Hopefully, with repetition and attention, we can find our way home. At the end of the day, we realise it's an inside job. It's also a process, and never happens as quickly or easily as we wish.

Mary Farrell has contributed her voice, heart, and years of professional experience to help in our journey of personal evolution. She won't promise results in 28 days, or in seven easy steps. She will, however, share her wisdom and enlightenment in the sincere hope that a more joyous and rewarding life may be realised.

Susan Winter

Introduction

Lighting the darkness

My purpose in writing this book is to look at the ways in which trust is built between us, how trust begins, how it develops and how, sometimes, it is destroyed. It seems to me that trust is the most significant part of the relationships we build with each other, and that without it there can be no true relationship. To trust is to relax. To trust is to be at peace and to enjoy our lives with a feeling of safety and well-being. For anyone who has wondered about how and why relationships succeed or fail, for the parents of children who wonder what they might offer the new generation, I hope to provide some food for thought. I don't believe in the quick fix or the magic bullet. We are infinitely intricate and fluid beings – to pin down or define human interaction is to belie our complexity. In terms of creativity, however, I believe that universal and relevant themes are restated in the stories, movies, plays, books, television programmes and popular songs that capture our imagination, and by exploring these themes I want to light a few candles in the darkness.

As a psychotherapist, I am aware of how many books have been written about psychology, relationships and child development. Difficulties we experience with each other can either be simplified in terms of formulas and advice – easy steps, bullet points, solutions to all your problems – or overcomplicated in terms of jargon and academic theories. Ideas from the world of psychology are all too often inaccessible or condescending. One of my main aims has been to clarify and explain the key ideas from some of the great psychological thinkers of the last 100 years: Sigmund Freud, Carl Gustav Jung, Heinz Kohut and Carl Rogers. Communication is one of the ways in which trust can be made or broken. You have trusted me enough to be interested in this book – communicating clearly and honestly with you, my reader, is my priority.

The birth of trust

When a baby is born, emerging from its own private heated swimming pool into the cold hard light of day, its first task is to learn to trust. The world that confronts that baby is full of sensations and scary strangeness. The baby depends totally on its caregiver. The mother of a baby is biologically predisposed to hold, cuddle and feed her child, and ideally, the bond between them is formed instantly and grows with every moment as they look at each other and have intense physical contact. However, if the situation is not ideal this bond can be disrupted by circumstance: sickness, relationship difficulties, psychological factors, poverty and, in the worst-case scenario, death of the mother, can prevent the prerequisites for trust from ever forming. The baby finds it impossible to rely on the regularity, love, warmth and safety that it so desperately needs to grow up into a healthy, confident child.

Are babies born trustful? According to recent research, certain monkeys have a predisposition to feel afraid, and a higher concentration of cortisol, the stress hormone, exists in their brains. It follows that people with this predisposition may have a much harder time accessing trust. Yet even the most trustful and least anxious child will learn, through stressful and traumatic experience, to feel fear when the triggers for trauma recur. So the child who has come into contact with a cold, unpredictable or cruel other will begin to have her confidence in others shaken and permanently eroded.

Trusting each other

As a psychotherapist, I see many stressed people. I am aware of the gift of trust that is daily offered to me. It is a frightening thing to talk to a stranger, especially when previous experience has indicated that other people are dangerous. Many of the patients who consult me have learned, through traumatic experience, to believe the lines of Carole King's famous song 'You've Got a Friend':

They'll use you, yes, and abuse you –
They'll take your soul if you let them

So how does it happen that fearful people seek out a stranger such as me, and trust me with their innermost fears, desires, dreams and memories – the most intimate details of their personal lives? I guess, firstly, they are reassured by my professional qualifications and memberships, and the code of ethics that governs my practice. The consulting room itself, with its calm and quiet atmosphere, becomes a kind of bubble – like that first warm pool of mother's womb – a different kind of space from the outside world. The quality of understanding and empathy offered by the therapist can soothe the fear and anxiety of reliving those awful memories.

Trusting a therapist or a doctor to handle our delicate psyches and bodies is a calculated risk. Boarding a plane flown by a pilot about whom we know nothing is a calculated risk. We are continually in the process of weighing up the odds when we calculate risk. Yet there are many people who ignore risk, flaunting their lack of care for consequence. 'Trust' is a word used so often that we rarely stop to question its meaning. Often applied to marital trust, it has become synonymous with the idea of fidelity – we say we trust our partners when we mean we believe they would not have an affair with someone else. However, sharing a living space with someone, eating and sleeping in the same house, implies that we also trust them with our safety. We trust them not to rob us of our possessions, not to poison us, not to murder us in our sleep. Alongside this trust runs the subterranean current of fear. Specific fear, triggered by unpleasant association, can become generalised fear in a context of threat.

Recent world events have brought home all too clearly how our trust in the safety of everyday reality can be shattered. The impact of the events of 9/11 proved beyond reasonable doubt that we can no longer rely on the idea that nothing will happen to us unless we are consciously aware of taking a risk. Circus performers, skydivers, mountaineers, base jumpers and stuntmen and women have seemed to be in a different category to the rest of us – they enjoy taking risks, flirting with death. Most of us know, in the rational and logical part of our brains, that the most risky thing we can do is to travel by car. The feeling, emotional part of us connects us with a sense of far greater risk when we travel by air. Although we know, again with the rational left brain area, that air travel has an unparalleled safety record, when we look at the great metal bird, holding its cargo of people and baggage, the whole thing just seems too unlikely.

This unease, of course, is bound to be exaggerated by the horrific hijackings that took place on 9/11. Who, other than a film director, could conceive of two planes flying a straight course into those famous twin towers? Who could imagine that thousands of people who just turned up for work in the office that morning would become charred corpses in scenes of carnage and devastation previously only seen in war zones? We learn from our experiences of life. We adapt our lives accordingly. We begin to fear the everyday routine we have previously taken for granted.

Shakespeare's riddle

'He's mad that trusts in the tameness of a wolf, a horse's health, a boy's love or a whore's oath.'

These words are spoken by the Fool in Shakespeare's *King Lear*, during the third act, when the suffering of the old king is at its peak. This is a play about trust. A king has reached the last years of his life, and asks each of his three daughters to make a speech of love to him, so that he can decide which one of them he will trust to look after him in his dotage. On the basis of their words he makes the wrong decision and trusts the two daughters who are easy and seductive with words. Sadly, they do not have his good at heart. The Fool, often played as a frail young boy or a very old man, is the king's beloved companion, his entertainer – he also seems to be a kind of spiritual guide, or mentor. In the madness that overtakes the demented King Lear, the Fool is the voice of sanity, yet he speaks only in enigmatic riddles. In this third act of the play a crazy mock trial is held in a barn out on the storm-blasted moors. Lear is accusing his evil daughters of their crimes. The Fool's words represent his final, vital message to Lear – he disappears shortly after speaking them, and we don't see him again. Later, much later, Lear tells us his poor Fool is dead.

What is the hidden wisdom in these last words? If a little wolf cub has been raised by a loving human, fed milk and meat by hand, and seems to be a docile pet around the house – loving, intelligent and responsive, would we be mad to assume its wild and primitive nature has been permanently quelled? The horse – Equus – is the essence of the wild and the free, yet we break horses in, subdue them, control them. To assess the physical health of the horse is one thing, but how do we gauge those factors vital to the rider – its mental and emotional health?

Can it ever be possible for men and women to trust each other? The boy's love, the whore's oath – perhaps these are caveats about the perils of trusting a member of the opposite sex. In my local cafe, the waitress wears a T-shirt bearing the slogan 'Boys Lie'. The women who come into the cafe always laugh knowingly when they see these words. As children, we are often let down and betrayed by the parent of the opposite sex. So many of the insults we commonly use are gender-based – 'whore', 'tart', 'dick', 'prick' – perhaps the way we speak of the opposite sex reveals the deep disillusion we feel when the parents we adore reveal their true colours. Mother leaves the little boy at kindergarten and abandons him, father distances himself more and more from his daughter as she reaches puberty. Worse still are the many incidents of repeated childhood abuse – what greater betrayal of trust can there be than a father who sexually abuses his little daughter? Are the words of the Fool simply about trusting the wrong person? Or are they about the fear of risking our lives, our bodies and hearts; the fear of becoming vulnerable, as we all were as children, and being ill-treated, scorned and betrayed?

The extreme variety

Risk and trust, close companions, are vividly portrayed in the lives of exceptional adventurers, performers, animal handlers and rescuers. In the first two chapters of this book I look at the lives of four such people, who have somehow managed to strike a balance and live with danger in peace and harmony. If we take risks without taking account of our vulnerable underbelly, then we play with danger in a reckless, self-destructive way. Yet what constitutes risk for one person can seem unworthy of consideration for another. The extreme sportsperson, the snow-boarder, the rock-climber, would find it hard to understand the agoraphobic who will not venture from the house. The man who falls wildly in love and proposes to his sweetheart within a few days of meeting her would be amazed at the cautious bachelor who waits for years before popping the question. Trust, risk, fear and consequence seem to be woven together in a tapestry of cultural rules, expectations and associations. I have attempted to unravel the strands of this tapestry by looking at individual experiences.

Trust in love

In the later chapters of the book, I explore the parts played by risk, fear and trust in our most intimate relationships and in our expectations of ourselves and of others. How does our early experience affect the levels of trust inside us as we grow into adults? How do traumatic incidents change our inner landscape into one that is ruled by suspicion, nervousness and constant vigilance? In the process of researching these matters, I have become aware of the pivotal nature of the concept of trust in so many of the stories I hear in the therapy room. Couples who have grappled with issues of trust, or the lack of it, seek therapy for their troubled relationships. So often, the issues go back to childhood neglect, or abuse. How does any man trust a 'whore's oath' – how does any woman trust the word of 'a boy'?

We fear each other; we fear our own emotional and physical fragility. Fear is closely related to trust, and may be seen as its opposite. We learn to fear by repeated unpleasant experiences. Most phobias are born in traumatic events. We all know that the 'once bitten, twice shy' rule makes a lot of sense. A man who goes out running early every morning will quickly learn where an aggressive dog is likely to run out and bite his ankle. He will feel a corresponding nervous anxiety, a rise in the levels of cortisol in his bloodstream as he approaches that place, and may change his route if the fear becomes intense. The betrayed wife, the deceived husband, will find it harder to trust another partner next time.

In the light of Shakespeare's words, put in the mouth of the wise fool, I have been inspired by the extraordinary level of trust shown by Rae Evening Earth Ott, as she shares her daily life with one of the most feared animals – the wolf. Ross and Elisa Hartzell are a married couple who defy death on a regular basis with their 'William Tell' circus act, shooting apples from each other's head. Franklin Levinson, the horse whisperer from Maui, perhaps knows more about a horse's health than anyone in the world. Susan Winter, co-author with Felicia Brings of the book *Older Women/Younger Men*, trusted me with her own, very personal experiences of love. Heterosexual and gay couples have told me the stories of their fantasies and relationships. Michael Hurst, a shining example of courage and creativity in the world of the theatre, shared his feelings about acting as well as his own personal history with me. Then there are the accounts of my patients, which I have blended into semi-fiction, based on real experiences. I express my heartfelt gratitude to those people who have allowed me to use their material in this book.

Chapter 1

The Tameness of a Wolf

For as long as frightening stories have been told to scare children on a dark night, the wolf has been the symbol of the primitive predator. Wily, vicious, tricky and malevolent Mr Wolf – the Big Bad Wolf – has pretended to be a friendly visitor to little pigs, and dressed up as a child's grandmother before devouring his victims with his big teeth. In the original version of the old tale of Red Riding Hood, Little Red Cap meets with a very seductive wolf. Perrault tells of a young girl meeting a quietly spoken and cautious wolf in the forest. She tells him the way to her grandmother's house, as he expresses a wish to go and see Grandmother too. When Little Red Cap arrives, the wolf has eaten Grandmother and is lying in her bed, naked. He invites the girl to join him. Red Cap undresses and is amazed at how Grandmother feels naked: 'What big arms you have,' she says. 'All the better to embrace you with,' smiles the aroused wolf. We all know how this story ends.

The deep fear we have of losing control of our impulses and appetites has somehow found its way to the image of the wolf. It has become for us the personification of unrestrained sexuality, greed and violence. These are the fearsome parts of ourselves we don't wish to own. We deny the existence of the deadly sins in ourselves – it is more comfortable to believe that we are wholly good and kindly disposed towards our fellow men and women.

Rae's story

In the small town of Conroe, outside Houston, in the US, Rae Evening

Earth Ott runs a wolf reservation, Sunkmanitutanka Oyate (Lakhota for 'People of the Wolf Nation'). Her view of wolves is a different one:

> You may be surprised to learn that wolves hear and pass high frequency information, like whales and dolphins. We still don't know what they do with this information, but it has been established that they do indeed make use of it. A wolf pack is a highly organised and complex social structure. Pack members live within a rigid hierarchy, and the rules of the hierarchy must be obeyed. This structure determines who will eat first, and thus ensures the safety and survival of the pack.

Far from being dominated by their appetites and impulses, the creatures Rae Evening Earth describes read body language carefully and minutely to preserve order within the pack and keep the peace between the different members. The 'alpha pair', the largest and most intelligent wolves, mate for life, and are, as a rule, the only members of the pack to produce offspring. It is the female wolf, rather than the male, who is the fastest and best hunter. It is believed that most packs are run by females. There seems no evidence that wolves are any more primitive, any more driven by their own impulses to kill or ravage than any other animal. In fact the wolf pack is governed by a high degree of internal organisation. Yet the myths and legends prevail. The wolf (and its metamorphosis into the werewolf) continues to be a symbol of ungoverned and rapacious appetite, preying on innocent human beings and ripping their vulnerable bodies to shreds in the depths of a moonlit forest.

How does it happen that, despite all this, a small and delicately built woman has chosen to spend her life among wolves? When I asked Rae Evening Earth to tell me about the circumstances of her birth and childhood, and about how her ideas of safety and trust developed, here is what she said:

The ideas of safety and trust weren't formed in me by the human species. I was the first born of the first born of the first born for several generations – and I was a grave disappointment. I wasn't a son. I spent my childhood seeing myself through the eyes of a man who didn't like himself very much – let alone me. He was a product of society. He was short and insecure and he moved from a position of fear. I was too young to realise that low self-esteem was a sickness – a fine example of the sins of the fathers, so to speak – just being passed on unwittingly.

I grew up in the 50s, when children were seen and not heard, and women were obedient little wives who took pride in cooking and cleaning – as if this defined their very existence. They did what their husbands told them to do. They had good, obedient little children, and they made happy homes. It was the era of silence. I call it that because no one talked about anything that might be considered unacceptable. Black people were called 'niggers' and Indians were about two notches below that. Half-breeds passed if they could and never mentioned skeletons in the closet. I grew up on the largest ostrich farm in the universe – everyone's remedy was the same – you stuck your head in the sand and pretended everything was OK.

Rae went on to describe to me a physically and verbally abusive childhood – her father took any opportunity to hurt her, and her Irish/German mother did not intervene. Her sense of belonging was almost non-existent. Where did she fit? Rae was genetically her father's child, a carbon-copy lookalike. She writes:

I was a wild Indian – you can't know how many times I heard that. I looked like my father. I hated him. Not for the countless times he shamed me, humiliated me, laughed at me, screamed at me, rejected me, hit me or hurt me. Not for any of those things … I hated him for not loving me. I hated him for making sure I understood beyond a shadow of a doubt that I was just unlovable.

From a psychological viewpoint, the outlook was bleak for a child growing up in such a climate. Without encouragement, reinforcement, acceptance and respect, the identity of the child cannot flourish as it should. The spirits of children are like little seedlings – they need feeding and protecting from the harsh elements. Damage to these delicate, growing beings, before they reach maturity, is likely to have lifelong effects, resulting in fragility of identity, lack of trust that things will turn out well, lack of trust in others, and lack of trust in the self.

The organismic self

The father of today's counselling theory, Carl Rogers, speaks of the 'organismic self' with which every child is born. This self is able to feel and experience without a critical censor, to express needs and feelings directly and without apology or excuse. After all, the newborn is a highly efficient mechanism for survival – if a baby needs feeding or warming, then that baby lets those needs be known in no uncertain terms. The baby doesn't preface its cries with anxiety about its mother's or father's needs – 'Maybe Mummy's tired or busy now – maybe she'll be angry if I make her come to me now – maybe she'll resent me for asking for food now – maybe she'll think I'm greedy.' However, as the baby grows into a child these anxieties enter into consciousness and start to have a huge influence on its interactions. If the child begins to associate expressing needs with a certain kind of behaviour very early in its life, those associations can last a lifetime. Rogers calls these associations 'conditions of worth'. The child learns, through direct and indirect messages from mother, father and other important figures, to behave in ways that conform to the rules, and gain it a feeling of being valued and respected by the powers that be. These rules vary from family to family, from culture to culture.

In his influential book *On Becoming a Person*, Carl Rogers writes of the need that develops as the child matures. This need is for what he calls 'positive regard'. In other words, it is the need to be valued, accepted and respected, which Rogers says is universal in human beings. At some point in our childhood this need becomes greater than our organismic needs. Rae Evening Earth's experience as a young girl was that approval was not on offer:

> I wasn't permitted to make mistakes or use bad judgement without being punished. I was a kid – he couldn't understand that. I wanted him to love me, and he didn't. For many, many years I thought I was just unlovable – it had to be me. I was somehow defective and no-one could ever love me.

When a child goes through such torment, Rogers describes a state of extreme anxiety emerging. The child's personal and individual experiences of herself, the needs of her organism and the world around her are in conflict with her need for approval. The growing child needs love and wants it, and discovers that certain behaviour will bring a loving response. However, when the child explores the world around her, she frequently encounters an adult response of 'No, naughty girl!' This can be accompanied by a slap or, as in Rae's case, by irrational, unjustified and painful physical punishment. Although she doesn't understand at first, she learns to associate the behaviour with the unpleasant reaction, and this happens over and over again. The behaviour might feel good to her, but slowly and surely her values are replaced by those of the adults around her. Sadly, in many cases the child's behaviour is not bad or wrong, but rather the natural curiosity of a little creature finding out about the universe. Rae describes this eloquently:

I experimented, I explored and invented. My parents said I was incorrigible – kinder people used words like 'free spirit'. My problem was simple – everyone wanted to teach me what to think, not how to think. I hated it – I rebelled against it with every fibre of my being. And I paid handsomely for it too. I spent long hours in my room, standing in corners, out in the hallway, in the Principal's office, and the closet. I spent just as many hours nursing bruises and crushed dreams. Trying to force me into being 'acceptable' was like trying to drive a square peg into a round hole. I got the message. I was just an ugly little dummy that nobody wanted.

The damage done

For most children in Rae's position, life becomes a self-fulfilling prophecy. Many live out what some psychologists call 'a tragic script', feeling at home only with other outsiders, often resorting to addictions to alcohol, food, drugs or sex to soothe them. The more damaged the childhood, the more the growing adult yearns for comfort. The poet Emily Dickinson, in these few succinct lines, describes the feeling common to many neglected children, who later become addicted to drugs, alcohol or sex:

The Heart asks Pleasure first,
And then, Excuse from Pain.
And then, those little Anodynes
That deaden Suffering –

However, Rae had a special way of comforting her wounded spirit – she had a calling, which became clear to her from when she was a very small child:

I know there might have been a time when I wasn't connected

with wolves, but I just can't remember it. Wolves lived in me, in my dreams and my thoughts, and they were never scary. They spoke to me in my mind and in my heart. They were my friends and protectors – they told me they would guard my spirit. I never mentioned the wolves to anyone. I trusted no-one. I'd learned at an early age that trust was synonymous with pain. I talked incessantly about everything. But never about the wolves. They were sacred and the most loving thing I'd ever know. I never told anyone about the wolves.

It was as if Rae was able to keep the most precious part of herself safe by her connection with the wolves. The idea of the wolves was her salvation. They became her secret, spiritual protectors. Every child needs to have ideal figures to whom they can look up – heroes and heroines. When we are small, these idealised figures are often our mother and father. We believe them to be omnipotent, omniscient. If, however, those parents, who should be helping us to become healthy adults, are actually damaging our potential, reducing our creativity and our ability to love and trust others, we must look elsewhere. Rae found the wolves.

The real thing

Rae's first encounter with a live wolf confirmed the extraordinary empathy and responsiveness that she had imagined in her fantasies:

I went to a place, many years ago, where they had a wolf. The manager of this place took us up to where this wolf was. His name was Lupe. He was lounging in front of his shelter under a tree. The manager told us not to get close, as the wolf would bite. He went on to explain this wolf had a temper and didn't like anyone. Even the people who feed and care for him lock him off in a separate section when they go in to clean and feed. I looked at the wolf. The group spread out along the fence line to have a better look. He watched them in contempt. I was mesmerised by him – not his beauty, although he was very beautiful, but by his spirit. I could feel him moving inside me. I walked to the front and bent down, twining my fingers through the fence to balance myself. Before the manager could say or do anything, the wolf got up and covered the ground between us. When he reached me, he stopped and abruptly locked me in his gaze. What I saw wasn't contempt any more, but a depth of sadness I had never imagined existed. His soul was crying. I saw his eyes soften and he began to lick my fingers. He took his front teeth and began to clean under each nail. His eyes were closed, and he looked peaceful. This was my brother. I was as sure of it as I am of my own existence.

Substitute family

Rae's feeling that she didn't belong anywhere was over. She had found her true family. She decided to devote her life to wolves somehow. This resolve was confirmed a few years later, when she was adopted by a Lakhota holy man, who became her spiritual guide. His name was Snow Eagle. Through this man, Rae learnt that she was worthy of love and respect. She was encouraged to make mistakes, and taught to embrace them. She learned to pay close attention to her emotions, and to understand what Snow Eagle taught her about the way human beings fulfil their own destinies: 'We all have this creative mechanism that fulfils our deepest beliefs. It will draw, like a magnet, anything you need to fulfil your vision. We are all self-fulfilling prophecies who become exactly what we think we are.'

Rae's creativity led her to find a substitute family – a family who would nurture her and feel for her in a way her own family was incapable of doing. As Richard Crashaw wrote four hundred years ago in his beautiful elegy, 'Hymn to St Teresa':

> Since 'tis not to be had at home,
> She'll travel to a martyrdom.

These words highlight the idea that, despite the inherent dangers and terrors embedded in a different kind of life, we will embrace them if we can find the acceptance, love and respect for which we have been yearning all our lives.

To be the self one truly is

Carl Rogers speaks of the goals that we have as we move towards an understanding of ourselves. In explaining how people often seek therapy in order to feel more whole, he uses Kierkegaard's words, as he describes the wish 'to be that self one truly is'. He describes how, in a climate of warmth, respect and safety, people tend to move away from the facade they have needed in the past, and to reveal themselves more honestly in their interactions. In an atmosphere that does not threaten to judge, criticise or punish, we leave the tyranny of the 'oughts and shoulds', and stop moulding ourselves into the people others wish us to be.

In the abusive situation, a small child is not only frightened into adopting a 'false self', but also becomes immensely skilled at reading body language and facial expression. A glance or a raised eyebrow can alert the child to potential danger to life and limb. The more tyrannical the adults, the more expert the child becomes at decoding the messages conveyed by non-verbal communication. The abused child is superb at guessing the mood of the abusing parent – she knows the instant the parent enters the room whether danger is imminent – her life depends on her extraordinary ability to read facial cues and body language. This ability, in turn, often informs the child's behaviour around the abusive adult. So it is that, far from being 'naughty' or 'bad', the child is simply attempting to survive and grow in a hostile climate. Rae describes this process exactly:

> He taught me to cover my tracks well. He taught me to lie, because if I told the truth I got punished. If I lied and didn't cover well, the punishment would be tenfold what it would have been had I just told the truth and took my licks.

Through her amazing ability to keep her inner core intact, Rae managed to survive her teens and twenties, when she 'ran with the wrong crowd' and felt desperately unhappy at times. The idea of the wolves never left her – they were welded to her spirit. She feels now that they taught her about safety and trust, about bravery and fearlessness. She feels that they are truly sacred beings, and in 1995 she created Sunkmanitutanka Oyate as a refuge for orphaned, abused and abandoned wolves. Most of the wolves and wolfdogs she rescues come from appalling situations – chained to trees, fenceposts or old refrigerators, covered in motor oil, stuffed into small pens, sick, alone, starving, beaten and forgotten.

Danger and acceptance

Rae is fully aware of the potential wolves have to defend themselves against perceived attack. She describes her first rescue of a young female wolf she called Cole. Cole was unsocialised and had been horribly abused. Rae and her partner, Marc, were building a habitat for Cole and some thirteen other wolves they had rescued. Cole was in a crate with a thin chain on her. Rae opened the door to the crate to give her some exercise, and Cole shot out like a bullet, the chain dragging on the ground behind her. As she rounded the other side of the shelter the chain caught on the corner and jerked her back:

I knew it hurt her and she was terrified, fighting it like a
wildcat. She was biting the chain repeatedly, and her teeth
were breaking. She was bleeding profusely from the mouth. I
knew Marc was too far away to hear me, and I also knew she
would hurt me if I intervened. She was powerful and she was
frantic. Wolves have about 1500 pounds psi in their jaws.

Although she was afraid for her life, Rae chose to help the young wolf.
She was bitten badly – a two-inch-deep, three-inch-round hole in her
arm. She saw to the wound herself, afraid that the incident would have
been reported had she gone to hospital, and that Cole would have
been destroyed. Her wound took three months to heal. She has no
regrets, and the event did not alter her feelings toward wolves:

I loved Cole. I still think about her. She didn't deserve what
happened to her. I'm glad she's free now. Trusting a wolf is
about letting go of your preconceived ideas and fears.
Allowing the wolf to teach you a better way.

The idea of taming a wolf is as ridiculous to Rae as the idea of taming
her next door neighbour. She sees wolves as her equals. Similarly, Carl
Rogers compares the natural inclinations of humans and animals
towards self-governing behaviour. He writes of the fear we have that if
we were to be allowed to become our true selves, it would mean that
we would be bad, destructive and uncontrolled, unleashing the beast
within us. He cites the lion as a symbol of 'the ravening beast'. Yet, as
Rogers writes in *On Becoming a Person*, when we look at the behaviour
of the lion – or the wolf – here is what we find:

He kills when he is hungry, but he does not go on a wild
rampage of killing, nor does he overfeed himself. He keeps
his handsome figure better than some of us. He is helpless
and dependent in puppyhood, but he moves from that to

independence. He does not cling to dependence. He is selfish and self-centred in infancy, but in adulthood, he shows a reasonable degree of co-operativeness, and feeds, cares for and protects his young. He satisfies his sexual desires, but this does not mean he goes on wild and lustful orgies. His various tendencies and urges have a harmony within him. He is, in some basic sense, a constructive and trustworthy member of the species *Felis leo.*

Carl Rogers and Rae Evening Earth share an understanding about people and animals. They believe that both human and animal species are well-intentioned, and if no trauma has happened to pervert their natures, people and animals tend towards mutual respect for each other and towards what Rogers refers to as 'the internal locus of evaluation' – in other words, the ability to rely on our own innate and intuitive values and meanings. The idea of trusting in the tameness of a wolf is perhaps more about the difficulty we have in trusting ourselves.

Chapter 2

The Wolf Within

The wolf appears to most children in their dreams. The cultural symbols of fear go in at a deep level, and haunt the unconscious. Dreams and nightmares play and replay as we sleep, reminding us of our insecurities and vulnerability. A language of the unconscious is formed in very early childhood, made up of images and metaphors we learn in our songs, stories, nursery rhymes and the words of our mothers and fathers. 'Who's afraid of the big bad wolf?' 'I'll huff and I'll puff and I'll blow your house down!' 'Oh Grandma, what big teeth you have!' – 'All the better to eat you with!' Such words go in at a hypnotic level when we are so little that we can only respond to them with the intensity of our feelings.

With the patients I see for therapy, a similar language often develops that belongs exclusively to the work. As the psychoanalyst Robert Hobson writes in his book *Forms of Feeling*:

> The process of psychotherapy involves a mode of artistic creation which has affinities with literature, music, drama, painting ... as a kind of partner in the creation of a shared feeling-language, the therapist needs to be a kind of artist. Being alone and yet together with his patient, he apprehends and co-operates with emerging forms of symbolism which are elaborated and organised as a unique personal conversation grows between them.

Vivienne

One of my patients, a highly intellectual and imaginative young woman (who I will call Vivienne) began to refer to her fears as wolves when we were in the process of uncovering the depth and darkness of her dreams. In one of these dreams, she stood inside a tiny, makeshift cabin in the woods. The trees around her were full of noises – the wind, animal sounds. The walls of the cabin were not solid, they moved and swayed. The light was changing from daylight to the deep blue of evening. She was alone. She was very small, and felt lost, 'like Gretel in the fairytale', she said. Cast out by the only parent she had, she was left to fend for herself and take shelter in this insubstantial dwelling. As the walls shook and trembled she felt she must leave the shelter and venture outside. By this time night had fallen, and as she stood outside the door of the cabin she saw hundreds of pairs of eyes glowing from the trees. She was surrounded by a pack of wolves. She woke screaming.

From that point on, wolves came to symbolise for her the unpredictable and terrifying nature of fate. In her work with me, the word 'wolf' became a 'code' word for irrational fears, which centred around her health. We spoke of 'healthwolves', when she spoke of becoming ill with cancer or other incurable diseases. Ironically, one of her greatest fears was of contracting the disease lupus – the name of this disease actually means 'wolf'. How do such fears become so ingrained in our psyches?

In a 1993 paper about trauma, a group of psychologists suggests that all of us develop convictions, or schemas, very early in our lives, about the nature of safety, trust, power, esteem and intimacy. These core beliefs are partly determined by the social and cultural climate in which we grow, and partly determined by our life experiences. As the psychologist Abraham Maslow wrote, to feel safe and secure is a basic human need and an important component of self-esteem. The baby needs to know and trust in the consistency and reliability of the care and nurture offered by family members. The growing child also needs to begin to trust herself as she explores and experiments in the world around her.

Donald Winnicott, a paediatrician and psychoanalyst who studied the behaviour of mothers and their small children, writes of 'the environmental mother' – the mother who waits and watches from the park bench while her exploring child discovers the joys of the playground. He can see her, and turns to her often to provide a feeling of security. He knows he can return to her if things become scary in any way – if he falls and hurts himself, she will be with him in a second. Yet she does not intrude. She is watchful, yet not interfering. She allows the child to become more confident, to trust himself.

Perhaps such children, growing in an environment of mutual trust and respect, learn a different kind of belief in themselves, and in their own ability to stay safe. It seems obvious that the child who grows up in a climate of physical, emotional, verbal or sexual abuse will have profound problems, particularly in the very basic and crucial areas of trust and safety. Yet what of those people who appear to have extraordinary faith in their own ability to stay in one piece no matter what the circumstances?

The Amazing Hartzells

Such a couple are 'The Amazing Hartzells', whose speciality is a highly polished 'William Tell' circus act, in which apples are placed on each of their heads. Ross Hartzell fires a single arrow at a crossbow which sends calibrations to two other crossbows, and arrows speed like bolts of lightning in a millisecond, piercing the apples, as the glamorous man and woman in their sequinned costumes stare resolutely forward. It is a truly amazing spectacle.

When I first got in touch with Ross Hartzell, a bizarre circus accident had just hit the news. In front of some 4500 spectators at a World Circus Festival in Paris, another circus couple had been about to perform the 'William Tell' act. Alain Jamet aimed his crossbow at the apple on his wife's head, and missed. The arrow struck Cathy Jamet just below the eye. Ross told me:

> From my experience, it is inconceivable for a shot to go that wrong. From the aimpoint of an apple shot being about three inches above one's head to a location under the subject's eye, that's about nine or ten inches. That is a very long way off target. I only hope that poor woman survives.

Cathy Jamet did survive, and last reports were that the 'Grey Arrow' act would be back on show before too long.

Although this amount of risk is inconceivable to most of us, there are famous and fatal instances of the 'William Tell' stunt having been attempted from time to time, outside of the skill and expertise of circus performers. The most notorious and chilling example is perhaps that of the 'beat generation' writer William Burroughs, who in 1951 killed his common-law wife, Joan, by attempting to shoot a tequila glass off her head. The scene is portrayed with horrifying realism in the recent film *Beat*. In December 2000, in Mexico, Adrian Quintana-Galindo placed a plastic cup on his friend's head and fired a single shot from a .25-calibre pistol. The bullet struck Manuel Dominguez-Quintero in the forehead, and he died instantly. Both these tragic incidents seem to have been attributable to the kind of false confidence in self that comes with the consumption of drugs or alcohol.

William Tell

The original William Tell story is one of true confidence, however, in the mastery of a specific skill. At the end of the thirteenth century, a petty, self-important tyrant called Gessler placed his hat in the marketplace of a town called Altdorf. He announced that every man who passed the marketplace should fall down on his knees and pay homage to the hat. One day William Tell, a hunter from a nearby valley, passed the marketplace with his son, and failed to fall to his knees. Gessler had him arrested and told him his only chance to stay alive was if, with a single arrow from his crossbow, he could hit the apple that Gessler placed on the head of his son. Unlike the previous examples, Tell's aim was accurate, and the arrow pierced the middle of the apple. Tell's second arrow went straight through the heart of the tyrant.

Ross the archer

Like the original Tell, Ross Hartzell is an expert marksman. He has learned to trust himself and his wife Elisa implicitly. When I asked him what the word 'trust' meant to him, here is what he said:

> I suppose it means something different to everyone. After all, it's your own emotion based on your own perceptions. On one hand, some people will be totally trusting of total strangers. Not necessarily to have them shoot apples off their head. But trusting enough to be taken advantage of. As you age, you learn not to be so trusting. As far as the type of trust involved in what I do, I don't think many people have developed it to the level that I have. Even if an unfortunate accident were to happen, it would not be for the lack of trust. Trust is something intangible that comes from within your own self. I trust my wife, in knowing that she would never cause me harm intentionally. I also trust my equipment in knowing that I have taken every precaution to ensure that things are calibrated correctly, and there is no damage or unacceptable wear to various parts. I am very particular as to the handling of my props. Even though I allow them to be handled by stagehands, I by no means trust them. I watch my equipment

like a hawk. So I guess you could say I trust myself, in knowing that none of my props leave my control. That's just taking care of business. I feel I have a firm grip on my feelings of trust.

In their publicity flyer, headed 'A Modern Day William Tell', Ross Hartzell describes his act with Elisa as follows: 'In a demonstration of ultimate trust, both performers take turns at being on the receiving end of speeding arrows, as they demonstrate unparalleled archery skills.'

As Ross describes, the trust involved between these two loving partners is extraordinary. He goes on to outline their relationship in the flyer:

To Ross, Elisa has long been the apple of his eye since they were both childhood sweethearts at the tender age of four years old, when their parents performed at the same circus. Thus formed the lifelong partnership that continues today.

Ross told me more about their early days:

As small children, we would ride the circus parade float together. The float was a take-off on a nursery rhyme – something about Inken, Winken, Blinken and Nod. I think we were dressed in nightgowns! We must have been about three years old.

They often saw each other and went out together in a crowd, but Ross and Lisa did not marry until they were well into their twenties:

Although we didn't know it at the time, Lisa and I were developing a great friendship. One day we realised we were in love. We had nothing but each other, and started our life together. I suppose our trust started to develop before that time, but it surely solidified during the next few years. She was a trapeze artist. Working without a net. I was responsible for the safety of her rigging, and also spotting for her while she was working. She completed her aerial career without having an accident.

Ross and Lisa's relationship has gone from strength to strength. They have learned, through many days and weeks of patience, care and dedication, to trust themselves and each other absolutely. In the environment in which Ross and Lisa grew from children to adults, trust has a sacred meaning. To guard another's life, as Ross did, watching Lisa's every move – the placing of her hands and feet, the exact angle of the arc of the trapeze, following her with the spotlight, checking, concentrating with every atom of his being – is the way of the circus. If your support people, your riggers, your technicians, your co-performers are not reliable and worthy of total trust, then quite simply, you are dead. Working without a net, as Lisa did, the performer's life is literally in the hands of her support workers.

Childhood beliefs

Beliefs related to our own decision-making ability play a crucial part in trusting others. Some children, it seems, grow up with the conviction that one can trust one's own perceptions and judgements. Others, particularly those who have been subjected to bad treatment, experience trust in themselves as a fragile quality, subject at any moment to attack from powerful others. Trust in ourselves can be shattered by traumatic experiences. Our own judgement is called into question.

As a child, Vivienne was repeatedly told that she was not to be trusted. The eldest of four children, she had had to take on the role of mother at just ten years old, when her mother left the family to live overseas with her new man. Vivi's father, instead of building a closer relationship with his children, distanced himself physically and psychologically by becoming more and more involved at work, leaving Vivi to become the caregiver of her three younger siblings. If anything went wrong – if there was an accident, a spill or a decision that Vivi was unable to make – she bore the blame. Her father, through his unreasonable expectations of his little girl, gave Vivi the unshakeable belief that she was fundamentally untrustworthy. Her experience of being cruelly abandoned by her mother, and emotionally stranded by her father, led to a mistrust of others, and of life itself. Worse than this, though, was the feeling that she could not trust herself.

People with severely damaged self-trust often have feelings of phobia, intense anxiety and confusion when confronted by situations that involve decision-making. So, Vivi's 'healthwolves' haunted her in her adult life whenever she had to decide whether or not she was unwell. A slight cold became a nightmare, a bout of food poisoning seemed life-threatening. How could she decide if she was going to make it through the night? Who would help her to contain her fears? She developed into a woman who spent most of her hard-earned wages on medical consultations, blood tests and alternative practitioners. Every time she looked out of her cabin windows, the wolves were watching and waiting. Her social isolation became a vicious cycle of deprivation and over-vigilance. As E.M. Forster writes in his novel *Howards End*:

> With infinite care we nerve ourselves for a crisis that never comes … We assume preparedness against danger is in itself a good, and that men, like nations, are the better for staggering through life fully armed. Life is indeed dangerous … it is indeed unmanageable, but the essence of it is not a battle.

If we see Vivi's wolves as being symbols of needless worry, we can see the toll this worry takes on her life. Constantly vigilant and hyperaroused, she is never sure of her own perceptions, never able to trust that she will feel better in the morning.

Embracing the wolf

Ross and Lisa's experience of danger is a different animal entirely. More like the wolves who nuzzle Rae's hands and drape themselves across her body to keep her warm when she spends the night with the pack, the everyday danger that accompanies these two people seems both beautiful and enriching.

As Forster goes on to say: 'Life is unmanageable because it is a romance, and its essence is romantic beauty.' Ross and Lisa's romance blossoms in a climate of danger and excitement – they grew up in such a climate. Lisa is the eighth generation of circus performers, Ross the third. They were nurtured in an atmosphere of love, care and an awareness of safety and danger made so much sharper by the work of the circus community:

> Of course our parents knew each other. Lisa came from a strict Italian family. Lisa's mother, when just a young girl was not allowed to talk with, or otherwise hang out with anyone other than my mother. My father made the rigging Lisa used early in her aerial career. We ourselves have always been the best of friends. Friendship first – the foundation of our marriage. She is the person in all the world I can trust with no limits. If she were to let me down, it would not be for lack of trust – it would be beyond her control. She already has my forgiveness. We always kiss just before we walk on stage.

It is not that Ross and Lisa are unprepared for the danger of what they are doing – far from it – they do all they can to maintain the absolute safety of their act. Ross described the origin of the act to me:

We started working on the archery act in the late seventies. We enjoyed it immensely – it just sort of developed. It all began when I was building a flintlock rifle from a kit. I wasn't very happy with the quality of the kit, so I returned it to the store, and ended up walking out with a bow and arrow set. I stopped at the ranch supply on the way home, and picked up four bales of straw to shoot into. I tested my archery skills, and found I had none. I consistently missed the bales of straw and launched arrows into the open fields behind my home. Despite the sore muscles and the lack of skill, I persisted. I took lessons from a man who used to be an exhibition shooter when he was young. As he knew our showbiz background, he enlightened me to some of the techniques we still use today. We worked long and hard to develop our craft. In fact we only attempted the apple shot after we had been working towards that moment for three years. We approach every shot we do very methodically, with safety always being our primary concern.

Like Rae, Ross and Lisa approach danger with the utmost respect, and take every precaution against tragic accident. The romantic beauty of the speeding arrows and the loving eyes of the wolf accompany their preparedness. They are afraid of real danger, rather than imaginary danger. Hippocrates, writing 2400 years ago, noticed that there were people who 'feared that which need not be feared'. Such people have grown up with the idea that life itself is a hostile medium – as children, such has been their experience. Others, like Ross and Lisa, have grown up in an atmosphere of love and protectiveness, despite the danger of what they do, and of what their parents did. Rae Evening Earth Ott has, through a significant reparative relationship and her own courage, faith and sense of vocation, managed to overcome the experience of having grown up in a hostile and destructive environment to such an extent that she lives in peace with the wolves.

The stories in this chapter bear witness to the fact that true trust must be based on the firmest foundations of security, confidence and faith. Through repeated experience of mutual trust, the wolf trusts the woman, the woman trusts the wolf. Through the experience of arrows that consistently hit the mark, the loving couple trust that they will come through unscathed. Trust can be destroyed – it can also be created and nurtured.

Chapter 3

Man and Horse

The intense connection between humans and horses began 50,000 years ago, when Cro-Magnon man started to use horses not only as food, but also as pack animals to assist in a nomadic way of life. Around 5000 years ago, horses began to be tamed for riding – unearthed horse teeth from this time show wear from a bit, the metal mouthpiece used to control the horse.

Millions of years ago North America was home to thousands of wild horses; perhaps it was a combination of man's treatment of them, predation, disease and environmental factors that led to their disappearance – by 8000 BC there were no horses left on the whole continent. It wasn't until the sixteenth century that horses returned to the Americas. The apocryphal tale of the first sight of the Spanish conquistadors and their horses is borne out by witness. Bernal Diaz de Castillo, companion to Cortes in his 1519 voyage to Mexico, wrote: 'The natives had never seen horses up to this time and thought the horse and rider were all one animal.' This sentence conveys the powerful idea of horse and human as a single being.

In 1541, Viceroy Mendoza put allied Aztec chieftains on horses to better lead their tribesmen into the Mixton War of Central Mexico. This seems to have been the first time horses were officially given to Indians, who were observed to rub themselves with the sweat of the horse to acquire the magic of the animal they called 'the big dog'. Magic indeed, for the great and beautiful partnership between the

American Indian and the Spanish horse gave the people an incalculable advantage – as hunters, as travellers, as traders and as warriors.

As the Ferrari or the Porsche represent the longings of today's human being to *become* the qualities that such a machine represents, so, for hundreds of years, the horse's speed, strength, beauty and majesty have not only been used by humankind, but also coveted. The experience of powerlessness engenders the longing for power. The following passage from J.R.R. Tolkien's *The Lord of the Rings* paints a picture of the fantasy so many children have – this is what isolated or neglected children might long for in their dreams – to merge with a beautiful, powerful creature and become one with it:

> Their horses were of great stature, strong and clean-limbed: their grey coats glistened, their long tails flowed in the wind, their manes were braided on their proud necks. The Men that rode them matched them well: tall and long-limbed; their hair flaxen-pale, flowed out under their light helms, and streamed in long braids behind them; their faces were stern and keen. In their hands were tall spears of ash, painted shields were slung at their backs, long swords were at their belts, their burnished shirts of mail hung down upon their knees.

Like the first view of the Conquistadors, this passage shows the horse and rider as one being, sharing the same beauty, the same power and majesty – the horse's qualities are absorbed by the human rider. The power of the horse is the power of the rider – the health and strength of the rider depend entirely on the health and strength of the horse.

Horse whisperer

At the age of 13, Franklin Levinson was already a skilled horseman. His father was a champion polo player, and Franklin grew up with a great affinity for horses. He has thought a great deal about trust:

Where do trust, safety, security and peace exist? They exist in feelings. Are we safe when riding in a car? It seems to me we are only as safe as we think we are. We can only have feelings of safety. So it might be said that trust and safety do not really exist outside of ourselves. It is an internal process and really does not exist in the world outside of our consciousness.

Today Franklin acts as facilitator, translator and teacher of what he calls 'Equus' – the language of the horse. Twenty years ago, he began his Adventures on Horseback trail ride, taking riders out to explore cliffs, bush and waterfalls in one of the most beautiful coastal areas of the world: Maui, Hawaii. Now he leaves that part of his work in the hands of his managers. For some time he has been accepting groups of children and disturbed adolescents from Child and Family Services in Hawaii, and other agencies, on his course 'The Maui Horse Whisperer Experience'. Although today his primary work involves running programmes that he calls 'The Way of the Horse', helping kids in need is an endeavour very close to his heart:

My childhood was anything but peaceful or filled with feelings of trust. My dad was a rageaholic. He was very unstable emotionally. It was hard for me, as a child, never having the feeling that everything was OK. Fortunately, my dad was into horses. Polo, to be more accurate. He liked the exercise he got from riding, and the glory and prestige that came from playing 'the sport of kings'. For me it opened up a world where trust and safety did exist within the relationships I was able to establish with our horses. From a very young age, horses would calm down when they were close to me.

As a child, Franklin yearned for a calm, safe and trusting atmosphere in which to grow. The horses responded to him, and he to them – he was able to give them exactly what he needed for himself. His instinctive understanding of the nature of the horse came directly from his experience as a frightened and powerless child:

> I believe horses are attracted to peace. Because it is a prey animal, always wary of the possibility of a predator nearby, it knows terror. Terror is the feeling of being helpless to save our lives in the presence of mortal danger. I look at the flight response of horses as moving to peace, rather than running from fear. They want that safe, peaceful feeling again, desperately.

Containing and understanding

Franklin's personal experience of terror, coupled with his articulate imagination, allowed him to empathise with his dad's horses. Somehow, even then, he could imagine himself into the horse's psyche. In 1968 the psychoanalyst Heinz Kohut wrote about the early developmental needs of children. He believed that empathy was the crucial element that needed to be present for children to grow up with a healthy sense of themselves and others. Empathy is a word that is often used but little understood. Not sympathy, not identification, empathy is a way of imagining how it feels to be another person. As Carl Rogers writes in *On Becoming a Person*, empathy has to be focused not on your feelings, but on those of the other person: 'To sense the other's fear and confusion as if it were your own, yet without your own fear and confusion getting bound up in it ...'

If a child is responded to empathically, then the child will flourish. Empathic understanding of the child's world means that we understand the needs the child has at different stages of life. It means that we can allow for the child's need to have a calm, containing adult who will accept the shifting moods that are inevitable for the still forming personality. Franklin describes the horse as a child, longing for this sense of safety: 'I like to think of horses as very large, very young children, infants, if you will, born pure, innocent, dependent – totally giving love and open to receiving love.'

Children shift very quickly from delight and happiness to fear and frustration, and Kohut, while accepting that no parent can be perfect, said that the small child needs to merge with the loving, soothing parent in order to begin to love and soothe itself. One of my own most treasured memories of my son's early childhood illustrates this process. My little boy, then about two years old, had had a bout of vomiting. It was the first time he had experienced the shock of this kind of reaction to food that had disagreed with him – different from the regurgitation of undigested food by a baby. He was naturally distressed as we sat in the bathroom together. I was stroking his head with a cool sponge, and saying to him gently, 'Poor baby! Poor baby!' He looked up at me, and put his arms around his own body. 'Poor baby …' he repeated to himself. He looked thoughtful, as if he had discovered something. 'Poor baby,' he went on saying gently to himself, as the distress lessened. He had absorbed, or internalised, my loving care for him, and could apply it to himself! In this way the child can gradually take in the qualities of the parent, strengthening the child's personality and preparing her for increased independence.

If, however, the parents are preoccupied with their own anxieties and unmet needs, and are unable to provide an empathic environment, the child will grow up with similar anxieties and unmet needs, unable to trust himself or others, and searching for an alternative ideal figure whose qualities might help him to become independent. This can be an alternative parent, like Snow Eagle, who became Rae Evening Earth's substitute father; it can be a hero or a heroine in a story; it can be an animal or even a toy. Often children, searching for a way to feel whole, will use a combination of the real and the imaginary to sustain and nurture them on their journey towards becoming a person.

The role of fantasy

In his book *The Uses of Enchantment,* Bruno Bettelheim, a psychologist and educator, writes of the importance of fantasy in the child's journey towards adulthood. Fairytale characters, journeys and miracles are resources to help the little child imagine herself as a good strong being, who can have good experiences. Stories, legends, songs and myths support the child in adding pictures and words to these imaginings. Bad experiences, on the other hand, are poisonous to the child, and the child wants to get rid of the difficult feelings associated with them – to spit them out. The anger, hostility and aggression felt by the child are, literally, projected out on to someone else – disowned – and mother becomes, temporarily, the Wicked Witch or the Bad Stepmother. Fairy tales are not ambivalent – characters are either good or bad, stupid or clever, beautiful or ugly. One parent is good, the other wicked. Children are often isolated and vulnerable, prey to the wicked opportunist, yet in fairy tales the bad person never wins. The message to the child is that the difficulties inherent in life are worth tolerating – the journey will have its terrors, but the happy ending will be reached. Often a magic animal – a wise lion, a great bird or friendly cat, a beautiful white horse or a unicorn with a golden horn – will accompany him along the most fearsome paths, or rescue him from the dragon in the nick of time.

Myths and fairytales, as Bettelheim says, '... answer the eternal questions – What is the world really like? How am I to live my life in it? How can I truly be myself?' From all the chaotic and intense feelings of childhood, meaning is formed by the messages we internalise from the adult world of fact and fiction. However, although written by adults, fairytales, taken as they are from ancient folk tales and parables, speak from the child's perspective. For the child, all things that move have life – animals who speak and think are a natural part of the child's inner world, and can impart wisdom and knowledge to the child. Above all, the child is searching for an identity, an answer to the question 'Who am I?'

The conscious world in which we all live resembles a frozen lake on which we are skating to and fro. We see each other gliding by, we are aware of the appearance of our skating clothes, the superior or inferior quality of our skates. We assess our skill at skating compared to that of others. The ice cracks here and there – we skate away, frightened. Yet underneath the fragile surface of the ice is a fathomless lake. In the lake live all kinds of beings and feelings, just like fairytale figures – the bad, the good, the beautiful and the ugly. Our dreams, with their strange and sometimes frightening symbols and metaphors, scare and fascinate us. Dream research has shown that people deprived of dreaming, even though not deprived of sleep, are impaired in their ability to manage reality; they are prone to confusion and hallucinatory images. The fathomless lake of our unconscious minds makes itself known to us in sleep, and if we pay attention to what has been revealed to us we can return to the real world better able to deal with the problems and conundrums of our daily life. We can know ourselves better. The symbols in fairytales can provide a kind of spiritual food in the same way, to help children progress towards self-knowledge and the strength to face the journey ahead of them.

When Franklin retreated from the world of his critical and unpredictable father, he found himself in the calm, magical world of horses. The horses seemed to sense that special part of him where his true spirit resides. He saw himself reflected in their loving eyes. They saw his soul – that was how it seemed, anyway:

> Horses are mystical creatures with magical qualities, innate dignity and a majestic nature. When a horse chooses to respond to you, it's magical – it's wonderful to have a 12,000-pound animal put his head in your lap, great for self-esteem issues. The horse acts as a kind of a mirror – whatever you bring is reflected back to you by the horse.

Franklin brought an inexhaustible supply of empathy to his dad's horses when he was a child, and it guides his work today, many years later. His main concern is to help people to understand the horse's natural and desperate desire to connect deeply with whoever is around it – horse or human.

Pony Boy

Franklin told me the story of a horse he called Pony Boy. The horse had been advertised for sale, and Franklin decided to make the trip to Honolulu to see him. The owner of the horse warned Franklin about the animal's meanness – that he kicked and bit and chased kids. Franklin went over to the pasture where Pony Boy was grazing with some other horses:

> I haven't chased a horse in a long time. I have discovered that if I let go of my agenda to 'catch' the horse, and have the intention to just be near the horses, they'll usually come over to me once they feel comfortable with that.

With perfectly pitched empathic attunement, Franklin imagined how it might be for this horse, and sat near him, without threatening him or invading his space in any way. Making 'sweet sounds – kisses and clucks and the like', Franklin waited until Pony Boy came to him.

> I led the horse back to where the owner was standing in amazement. Next, I began touching the horse all over to see where he was sensitive. He pinned his ears back (a sign of fear and displeasure) almost immediately. I just talked soothingly and calmly, and did my best not to push his boundaries too much.

Franklin bought Pony Boy and took him back to Maui. He learned more about this horse.

Once there was a rider on him, he was perfect – I could put little children on him, and he was great. He always seemed stressed out when people were near him on the ground. He would clench his teeth and tighten up, ring his tail, pin his ears and show signs of nervousness and fear. About this time, he had a bout of colic. Colic can be brought on by nerves. Diana, my ranch manager, her husband, my wife and I took turns staying up all night and holding his head and stroking him or walking him around so he wouldn't thrash about on the ground. We all tried to reassure him he was loved and cared for and didn't need to feel afraid. We offered him peace. He finally rallied. Since then, Diana praises him daily – she holds his head, strokes him a lot and speaks lovingly to him. We all do. Sure enough, the little guy has rebounded amazingly well. I know this horse was abused severely in his early days. That is how horses become dangerous (people too). They think they need to get to people before people get to them. Let's be peace bringers, let's extend love and peace and help to those who are sick, in pain and are acting out of fear. Perhaps they can learn to trust again, like Pony Boy.

The parent's role

Franklin has offered his horses the very environment he was denied as a young child. The peace, caring and love, the respect for boundaries, the 'sweet sounds' of affection and warmth were sadly lacking as he grew into a teenager. He speaks movingly of the horse's deep desire for the presence of an 'alpha leader' for the herd:

The true alpha leader for the horse herd is like Gandhi. The great, gentle, all-knowledgeable, compassionate leader who does not bully or threaten or bribe, but rather, like Gandhi, embodies wisdom, quiet strength and great leadership. The true alpha leader is not challenged by younger horses – they protect and revere her, as their survival is her survival.

Franklin is aware of the parallels between horse and human longings – the longing of every child for the ideal parent. He calls the alpha 'the great parent – the embodiment of all that is good, great, wonderful, wise, compassionate, powerful – and at the same time gentle'. This description is worlds away from his own weak, aggressive and unempathic father. His mother was also unable to take this role. Overwhelmed by the intense battle between herself and her husband, she withdrew emotionally from him and from her growing child:

> Things were so awful when I was growing up, and they were battling so much, she and I never really had the chance to develop our relationship all that much. They used to play me one against the other. I really don't think either one of them wanted to have kids. It was only after my father died that she and I became close and remained that way until the end of her life.

Despite the grim and desolate emotional landscape in which he grew up, Franklin managed to develop his own relationships with the animals and people who would give him the hope and determination to carry on. Sadly, there are other children who never manage to find good parenting. These are the children for whom the future is bleak. Without any kind of adult model of love and kindness, without a true hero or heroine to guide and encourage, such an isolated child can become engulfed in his own vivid imagination.

Chapter 4

Equus: The Horse God

In June 1973, an extraordinary play exploded onto the London stage. Its subject matter could not have been more shocking. It was about a boy who blinded six horses with a metal spike. The play was called *Equus*, and it was written by that master craftsman of theatre, Peter Shaffer. Here is the note that Shaffer used as an introduction to the play:

> One weekend, I was driving with a friend through bleak countryside. We passed a stable. Suddenly he was reminded of an alarming crime which he had heard about at a dinner party in London. He knew only one horrible detail, and his complete mention of it could have lasted barely a minute – but it was enough to arouse in me an intense fascination. The act had been committed several years before by a highly disturbed young man. It had deeply shocked a local bench of magistrates. It lacked, finally, any coherent explanation. A few months later, my friend died. I could not verify what he had said to me. He had given me no name, no place, and no time. All I possessed was his report of a dreadful event and the feeling it engendered in me. I knew very strongly that I wanted to interpret it in some entirely personal way. I had to create a mental world in which the deed could be made comprehensible.

Indeed Shaffer did create the mental world of the boy he called Alan Strang and, perhaps even more intensely, he created the world of the boy's exceptional psychiatrist, Martin Dysart. Through enormous patience, sensitivity and skill, Dysart painstakingly uncovers the horror and ecstasy of Alan's inner life. It's a process comparable to that of an archaeologist working away with his delicate little brush, exposing ancient material. What comes to light is the crucial relationship between the boy and his mother. Mrs Strang is a barely held together person, whose state of mind is so fragile that she is ill-equipped to bring up the passionate and feeling young man in her care. Her empty marriage, repressed sexuality and obsessive preoccupation with the Bible lead her into an unhealthy, anxious over-involvement with her son.

Like many repressed and frightened people, Dora Strang has an eloquent imagination. She sees it all, describes it all, and impresses on the growing child the vivid pictures inside her head. Underneath her cultivated manners, her airs and graces, Dora is drawn by images of animal power and sexuality: 'Mum likes equitation – bowler hats and jodhpurs!'

> My name is Prince, and I'm a Prince among horses! Only my young master can ride me! Anyone else, I'll throw off! And then I remember I used to tell him a funny thing about falling off horses. Did you know that when Christian cavalry first appeared in the New World, the pagans thought horse and rider were one person?

It transpires that at the very time that Alan reaches puberty and becomes sexually aware, Dora's images and Bible readings find their way into his universe in a way that contaminates his normal development. He becomes unable to separate his sexual feelings from the sacred and godlike qualities of the horse, and the horse-god Equus becomes an exciting and terrifying object for him.

Dora: The Book of Job. Such a noble passage – you know
'Hast thou given the horse strength?'
Alan: 'Hast thou clothed his neck with thunder?'
Dora: 'The glory of his nostrils is terrible!'
Alan: 'He swallows the ground with fierceness and rage!'
Dora: 'He saith among the trumpets –'
Alan (trumpeting): Ha! Ha! Ha! Ha!

The ego

The psychoanalyst Sigmund Freud first mooted the idea that we develop a self – an idea of who we are – as we journey through childhood. He called it 'the ego'. When Freud first used this term it did not mean that we have an inflated idea of ourselves, just that we have a concept of what differentiates us from others, what makes us individual. William James, writing before Freud, called it 'all that a person is tempted to call "me" or "mine" '. It has also been defined as 'what I think of myself, what I value, what is mine and what I identify with'. Crucial to the development of self is the way in which we are defined, responded to and spoken about by the significant people around us. If we are seen as powerful and intelligent, we absorb that idea, and it strengthens our own view of ourselves. If we are seen as stupid and clumsy, we lose hope and faith in our own grace and ability. Sometimes, parents are so preoccupied with their own anxieties and aspirations that their children become almost invisible to them. Children in this situation are used by their parents as suppliers of limitless attention and admiration. Rather than the parent acting as a mirror for the growing child, helping the child to develop a sense of her own identity, the parent demands that life-giving mirroring from the child. The child gives it, because more than anything else, as little children, we wish to please our parents. Other children are forced into giving their parents a response that somehow satisfies a lust for power.

Christiane F

Christiane F, in her tragic story *Autobiography of a Street Girl and Heroin Addict*, describes this process eloquently. Her violent father would come home late at night, after drinking:

> Any little thing would send him off on a rampage. It might be toys or clothes that we had left lying around. My father always said the most important thing in life was to be neat and tidy. And if he found any untidiness when he got home, he would drag me out of bed and give me a beating. My little sister got the tail end of it. Then my father threw all our things onto the floor and ordered us to put them all away neatly in five minutes. We usually didn't manage it in that short a time, and so we got another flogging. My mother usually stood at the door crying while this was going on. She didn't dare to intervene because then he would hit her too. I somehow loved and respected my father in spite of all this. He towered above other fathers in my eyes. More than anything, I was afraid of him.

As an adult, looking back, Christiane could see that her father wielded such power over the family because 'he simply wasn't making it. He kept trying to get ahead and falling flat on his face. His father despised him for it.' Despite his dreadful treatment of her, Christiane continued to keep her father good, to feel proud of him, to offer him the admiration and adoration he could not find anywhere else. 'I never hated him, but was just afraid of him. I was always proud of him too. Because he loved animals, and because he had such a terrific car, his '62 Porsche.'

The influence of mother

Dora Strang uses Alan in a far more subtle way. She uses him as a disciple in her very own cult of evangelical fervour. Escaping from her lifeless marriage, she excites and arouses herself by reading passages from the Bible to her little boy. Dora's version of the horse becomes a vivid part of Alan's inner landscape, inextricably linked with his own growing sexual feelings. His father reports to Dr Dysart that he has seen Alan conducting a strange ritual in his bedroom, chanting in front of a big picture of a horse. The image of the white horse had replaced another picture, of Jesus on his way to Calvary:

> The Christ was loaded down with chains and the centurions were really laying on the stripes. He absolutely fell in love with it. He insisted on buying it with his pocket money and hanging it at the foot of the bed where he could see it last thing at night.

Alan is chanting a litany created in his child's imagination from the words his mother has read to him – words from the Bible mixed with fairy tale and nursery rhyme, pouring out in a chaotic stream:

> Prince begat Prince! And Prance begat Prankus! Flankus begat Spankus! And Spankus begat Spunkus the Great, who lived three score years! Leckwus begat Neckwus, and Neckwus begat Fleckwus the King of Spit. And Fleckwus spoke out of his chinkle-chankle!

The ceremony ends with Alan raising his head in a kind of ecstasy, and saying these words: 'Behold – I give you Equus, my only begotten son!'

Alan's confusion between his mother's bizarre representation of the Bible and his own growing passion for horses has a horrible outcome. He begins to work at a local stable, never riding the horses by day, but galloping off at night, naked and in secret, to the 'Fields of Ha-Ha' where he rides his horse in a passionate and masturbatory frenzy:

The King rides out on Equus, mightiest of horses. Only I can ride him. He lets me turn him this way and that. His neck comes out of my body. It lifts in the dark. Equus, my Godslave! Tonight we ride against them all!

Eventually, tragically, the terrifying and majestic horse god, who sees everything, witnesses his first, fumbling attempt to respond to his first girlfriend at the stables. Alan hears the words of the Bible coming from the horse's mouth, sees the betrayal and condemnation in its eyes and the terrible crime takes place. Alan's overwhelming fear of being judged and condemned by Equus for his ordinary sexual desire for a young woman leads him to a horrific act of violence. He strikes out the horses' eyes so that they can no longer see his sins.

What is psychological health?

The question at the core of the play seems to be 'What is health?' Has Alan, in his delusional state, somehow made contact with real ecstasy? 'With one particular horse, Nugget, he embraces. He showed me how he stands with it afterwards in the night, one hand on its chest, one on its neck, like a frozen tango dancer, inhaling its cold sweet breath.'

The truth seems to be that Alan has been used by his mother, and ignored by his father. What Dysart sees as Alan's ecstasy is the excruciating pain of a self that has been invaded by another's insanity. Alan's illness could be called schizophrenia – the label for a fragmented self, prone to delusions, hearing voices, seeing things. It could be called an hysterical fugue state, in which a person might dissociate from reality, and end up doing something unthinkable without any memory of having done it. It could be called 'folie à deux', the label given to a mental illness that has been induced in a fragile mind by a stronger and more powerful person. Whatever the label we apply, the result is that Alan has broken the rules of our society in a major way and his dreadful imaginings have become a crime.

The idea that people are 'natural born killers' is refuted by many reputable psychiatrists. Dr Edward Hyman, in his on-line interview 'Little Killers', says:

> There's simply no evidence available to us in science that there is anything such as a natural born killer. There are many people who would like to assert – a few of them in science, many of them in religious or political arenas – that violent children are not merely natural born killers, but some kind of super-feral predators. But there's no indication that this is a reality in any systematic research.

Rather, Dr Hyman asserts, violent children emerge from a background characterised by coldness, distance and lack of respect for the boundaries of the child and the physical and emotional vulnerability of the child.

> When we look at kids who've become violent, we often point to lack of empathy as something we want to be concerned with. And certainly in adults, an abjectly poor lack of empathy is something we see in the psychopathic syndrome – in a real psychopath who engages often in violent and very destructive behaviour ... But if we look at empathy, certainly in children, often what we're looking at is that when a person was a child, was that person the subject of empathy? Was that person allowed to have understanding, empathic interactions? And we've observed – we've done many studies on this – that the incapacity to develop empathy is a social phenomenon in a family where there is no empathy for that child.

How did it happen, then, that Franklin Levinson became the wise, loving and compassionate man he is today? In the cold and unpredictable world in which he grew up, there was little empathy:

> As a young boy of seven or eight years old, I was so unhappy and traumatized by my dad's rage, I remember spending a lot of time looking out of my bedroom window up at the stars and thinking that there must be a better way, that this way of living in turmoil and anxiety was not the only way for life to be. I remember thinking that if this was all there was then I didn't want to live at all. In fact I tried to end my life two times as a child. I was about ten or eleven years old. One time I ingested 20 Anacin and 16 Bufferin. A second time I drank iodine.

Like Rae Evening Earth, Franklin found the soothing and comforting he needed so desperately with the accepting, loving animals who seemed to recognise his fine spirit. Like Rae, Franklin also found a substitute parent who provided those 'understanding, empathic interactions' he so badly needed:

> I was lucky – I survived my efforts to end it all. At sixteen years of age, I met a person, the first of many, who showed me there were other paradigms for living. That life was actually meant to be a joyful experience, where love and peace existed together in the heart. This person was a woman who lived in a log cabin in the woods of Southern Michigan. She was a folk singer, spoke and sang in four languages, had dogs, monkeys, cats and other critters around her cabin. To me she was the most wonderful person in the world, and she loved me just as I was. I needed to do nothing to win her love. She extended it freely, and that helped me begin to see my own, true, lovable nature. People show up in our lives when we are ready for them, I guess. At sixteen years of age, with two suicide attempts behind me, I was ready ...

Before the nurturing good mirror of Rowena's unconditional love told him he was a valuable person, Franklin went to his father's horses as a child in need. Today, he sees the horse as that child:

> The horse is just like our young child, only it weighs 1200 pounds and is heavily armed. Yet it is still our child, and we need to find ways of getting its trust and respect, and be able to parent it and work with it and lead it. 'The Way of the Horse' is a guide for living an impeccable life, just like the true alpha in the wild horse herd. What parent doesn't want to be the great parent for his child?

The longing for the 'great parent' threads its way through the lives of those of us who were not well-parented. Franklin's exceptional ability to 'parent' his horses is firmly rooted in trust:

> There was something about me that helped them to feel that they could trust that they were safe when they were with me. Perhaps it was to do with the fact that I had no agenda when I was with them, other than to have an enjoyable experience. Feelings of trust happen for kids and horses from appropriate guidance and support. In the case of children, that usually comes from parents. For the domesticated horse, it is supposed to come from the humans who have the responsibility of caring for the horse. Calmness and safety – I instinctively knew these were important for the horse, even though I still wasn't aware of how important they were for me.

Is it mad to trust a horse's health? Franklin believes a horse's health is dependent on the health of the owner.

> Horses are totally honest. They never lie. They are incapable of it. If horses look sick, they are. I think the statement about

not being able to trust a horse's health actually means more about trusting the human who is telling you about how healthy their horse is.

Projection

Just as the unempathic, distanced parent will have little idea of the state of health of his child, so the horse-owner who only wants to make use of his horse will be out of touch with the condition of his animal. What can also happen is that children and animals can become unwitting vessels, used to store all the unwanted qualities and attributes of the parent. The psychoanalytic term 'projection' is used to describe a process that occurs below our conscious level of everyday dealings. There are feelings we would rather not own, feelings we have been trained to repress – envy, covetousness, pride, lust and aggression, greed and sloth – the seven deadly sins. In a culture that highly prizes nobility, self-sacrifice, containment and 'goodness', it is natural enough that we fear being seen as 'bad', 'greedy', 'spiteful' people. The seven deadly sins in all of us are usually put away in the deepest cupboard of our minds, and the door is locked. What happens next in the process is that we see these qualities, the very qualities we are seeking to disown, in others. Children and animals are powerless to resist our definitions of them, as our mirroring is vital to their growth and development.

Martin's story
A patient of mine, who I will call Martin, is an elegant, graceful young man with striking good looks. Martin's father was the local butcher in a small village in Scotland, where everyone knew everyone else. This man had an obsessive hatred of homosexuality and, like many homophobic people, was terrified that his own normal feelings of affection for his male friends might be suspect in some way. His

longing for company and closeness with members of the same sex horrified him. In his turn, he had been treated badly by a physically abusive father, who had humiliated him repeatedly for the least little thing. His self-esteem was very low; he saw his body as large and lumbering and his face as ugly. As his little son grew from a baby into a child, and began to show his natural delicacy and sensitivity, Martin's father grew more and more anxious. What would happen if the people in the village thought Martin to be effeminate?

This man was not a cruel parent, insofar as he did not punish Martin physically, as he himself had been punished. He tried to be kind to the boy, and enjoyed their outings together. However, in the stories he decided to read to his little boy at bedtime, Martin's father would substitute Martin's name for the name of any characters who were big, bad or ugly. Monsters, bogeymen, dinosaurs and evil-doers were all called Martin. In this way, Martin's dad believed that he could train Martin to 'be more of a man'. Below the level of conscious thought he was ejecting his own unwanted view of himself as ugly, monstrous and aggressive, and attributing these qualities to Martin. As a consequence, Martin grew up believing there was something profoundly wrong with him, although he wasn't sure quite what it was. Rather than following a path into a career that would fulfil him, Martin forced himself into taking casual work on building sites – 'man's work' – where he felt depressed, alienated and often mocked by the other men for his slight physical build and sensitive ways.

In just the same way, we project onto our animals the qualities that either we do not wish to own, or those we wish we had. We idealise them or denigrate them. In *Apocalypse*, D.H. Lawrence uses vivid imagery to characterise the idealisation of the horse:

> How the horse dominated the mind of the early races! You were a lord if you had a horse. Far back, far back in our dark soul, the horse prances! The horse! The horse! The symbol of surging potency and power of movement, of action, in man!

When we denigrate the horse, it can be seen as lazy and stupid – a slave who must obey our commands to the letter, a beast of burden. The old Grimm fairytale 'The Fox and the Horse' illustrates this well. The story is about a faithful horse who had been a good slave to his master. The horse becomes old, and the master won't give him anything more to eat. He casts the horse out into the forest, with the insane requirement that the horse must show himself strong enough to bring home a lion.

> Alas, says the horse, avarice and fidelity dwell not in the same house together; my master has forgotten all the services which I have rendered him for so many years, and because I am unable now to work any longer, he will not give me any fodder, but has driven me out of the stable.

Only when the horse has proved his strength, vitality and resourcefulness by bringing home the lion (with a little help from his friend, the wily fox) does the master relent and take him in once more. In such a way, Martin's father was implicitly asking him to become a big strong brute of a man in order to prove himself worthy of love and acceptance. Martin has absorbed his father's confusion and self-denigration – he has devalued his own innate ways of being, living and loving, as his father did.

As an adult, Martin often finds himself in tears at the movies when he sees horses running across the screen, with their grace, freedom and beauty. For him, they represent all that he cannot allow himself to be. He projects onto the horse his own unfulfilled wishes and aspirations. On the internet, he has found a website about horses and unicorns. The following passage, about the creation of the first horse, moved him very much, and he brought it to a session to read to me:

> The bubble of light parted to admit him and then closed again. It spilled around him like liquid, and he felt himself changing. Strength flowed into him and fired his limbs, filled

out his body, raised his lengthening neck into a proud arch.
The magic parted, leaving the first horse standing trembling
between the two Unicorns. He was as golden as the rising
sun, with a creamy mane and tail. He reared and gave a
silvery cry that echoed down the valley.

If only Martin could have been allowed to develop into the golden,
magical, graceful self that he could have been without his father's
interference. The mirroring experience, faulty in his case, could have
been so different had his father been aware of what Martin needed
from him – recognition of his unique capacities, talents, abilities and
personal attractiveness.

A horse's health

Just as we see our children through the filter of our own frustrations,
wishes and unmet needs, so our animals become identified with the
particular attributes of our own life experience. The horse's health is a
mirror of our own. Only when we are healthy enough to appreciate the
horse as a separate and independent being, with very particular needs
and behaviour of its own, can we trust ourselves with its care. First we
have to free the image of the horse from idealisation or denigration.

Care of children and animals is a daunting responsibility. Only by
realising the huge task that we have in front of us, by facing up to our
own demons and fears, can we meet the task with integrity. If we avoid
this responsibility, how can we trust our horses or our children to be
strong and healthy? Health cannot be present when people or animals
have been used as slaves or whipping boys. To feel healthy, first we
must feel safe. In Franklin's words:

It seems that in order to give a horse a sense of safety and
peace we have to find it within ourselves first. I have found

this to be especially true when working with the troubled teens that come to my ranch. Part of what I ask them to do is to help the horse feel safe with them, to trust them. When they help the horse to feel safe and calm, they feel safer and calmer too.

The emotional, and perhaps the physical, health of those less powerful than adult human beings – the young and the dependent – can only be fostered by true empathy, respect and acceptance. These are the qualities of the 'great parent', who has learned self-knowledge and self-respect. As Franklin says:

I think earning the trust of the horse helps us to trust ourselves. Like the 'great parent' – always trustworthy for the child – by being trustworthy for the horse, we learn more about the nature of trust and how to trust ourselves.

Chapter 5

A Boy's Love

My class of counselling skills students was a bright bunch of educated adults, who had read widely about self-development. 'What do you know about Freud?' I asked them. In response, there were giggles and embarrassed glances. 'It's all about sex,' one of the students said. 'How so?' I asked. More giggles ensued. 'About snakes and penises and boys falling in love with their mothers,' came the answer.

The image of the Austrian psychoanalyst, with his funny accent, little glasses, his waistcoat and his beard and moustache, has been as widely parodied in advertisements and cartoons as the Mona Lisa and, like the smiling lady, the name has become a household word. The idea of Freud that seems to be most prevalent is that he was a slightly mad, voyeuristic and incomprehensible foreigner who was obsessed with sex.

In fact, Freud was born in Moravia in the Czech Republic in 1856. When he was three, his family moved to Vienna, and there he stayed until the Nazi persecution of Jews forced him to escape to England, where he stayed until his death in 1939. He studied physiology at the University of Vienna, and qualified as a medical doctor in 1881. The area in which he took most interest was the anatomy of the brain. This interest expanded in 1885, when he won a scholarship to travel to Paris and study with the famous Doctor Charcot, whose hospital for 'nervous diseases' was one of the first of its kind. Here, Freud observed the charismatic Charcot working with hypnosis to treat distressed patients. Freud began to consider and investigate the workings of the mind. When he returned to Vienna in 1886, he set up in private practice as a consultant in nervous diseases.

The great innovation brought into being by Freud during his lifetime of practice, research, writing and observing, was what he called 'the talking cure'. Rejecting the clinical use of hypnosis, Freud chose to ask his patients simply to say whatever came into their heads. This came to be known as 'free association'. In its turn, this led Freud to observe that while things would progress very well for a while, sooner or later the patient's stream of free association would dry up, and the cure would reach a temporary halt. He called this hiatus in the cure 'resistance'. In other words, the flow of images and desires that came tumbling out in the free association would be stopped by the patient's deep and buried fear of revealing too much to the psychoanalyst. Freud decided that this resistance came from the part of the patient's mind that he called 'the unconscious'.

The unconscious could be compared to a cellar or an attic, separate from the rest of the house, where our earliest memories and feelings have been stored. Our conscious mind is like the body of the house, where we live for most of the time, relying on our intellect, logic, experience and memories to make sense of what goes on – the comings and goings of daily life, the interactions of work and leisure. In cellars and attics, though, are the dusty trunks and boxes that hold long-forgotten memories and dreams, toys from our childhood, baby clothes and letters tied with ribbon. This is the world to which we travel when we dream.

In dreams, Freud believed, the true language of the unconscious is whispered in images that are only partly comprehensible to our conscious minds. Messages from the attic or the cellar are sometimes indecipherable, sometimes shocking, sometimes comical, sometimes terrifying. Our dreams hint at the pain and difficulty we have in facing ourselves, and the existence of the seven deadly sins inside us all. They hint at the terror we have of the hostility we might feel towards others

– the murderous feelings aroused by disempowerment or wounding – and the hostility others might feel towards us. They hint at our vulnerability and longing for closeness, and sexual longings we might experience for what seem the most unlikely partners. A common phenomenon in the course of psychotherapy is that the patient dreams of having sex with the therapist. Nowhere is this better illustrated than in the sensitive portrayal of the patient/therapist relationship in television's *The Sopranos*. Tony Soprano – the lewd, rough, overweight sociopath – dreams often and graphically of having sex with the reserved, intellectual, bespectacled Dr Jennifer Melfi.

The Oedipus complex

Freud's belief was that the ancient Greek myth of Oedipus held the key to many of our difficulties in adult relationships. Tom Lehrer, the American folk singer, puts it succinctly:

> There once lived a man called Oedipus Rex.
> You must have heard of his odd complex.
> His name appears in Freud's index
> Because he loved his mother ...

The story of Oedipus Rex was first staged in Athens in 425 BC. A central feature of the story is the character of the Oracle. At Delphi, in southern Greece, was a temple dedicated to the god Apollo. Inside the temple was a small underground cavern, where a specially trained woman responded to questions with prophecy. The vapours and mist she breathed from the warm spring beneath the temple would enhance the trance state from which she spoke. Oracles spoke at Delphi for a thousand years, were believed to be inspired by Apollo himself, and had huge power and political influence. The words of the Oracle were given total credence. The role of the Oracle was virtually identical to that of the Precogs in Steven Spielberg's 2002 blockbuster *Minority Report*, where specially gifted children are kept half-sleeping in a subterranean pool under the headquarters of the 'Precrime Division' and predict murders that are about to happen.

Laius, the King of Thebes, is told by the Oracle that his baby son will grow up to murder him. To prevent this happening, Laius and his wife Jocasta pin the poor baby's feet together and give him to a slave to carry out to a mountain where he is to be left to be eaten by wild animals. The slave takes pity on the little boy, and instead of fulfilling his horrible task he gives the baby to a friend who lives on the other side of the mountain in a country called Corinth. This man, in his turn, gives the baby to Polybus, the King of Corinth, who is unable to have children of his own. Polybus adopts the baby and calls him Oedipus – which literally means 'swollen foot' – because of the scarring and wounding of his feet.

Eighteen years later, someone at a party calls the young Oedipus a bastard. He is deeply insulted and leaves Corinth to consult the Oracle about the truth of his birth. The Oracle confirms the original prediction that he will murder his father and make love to his mother. Of course, at this stage Oedipus has no idea of his true parentage, and believes his father to be the King of Corinth. He is terrified by the Oracle's prediction, and moves away from Corinth, so that he cannot be anywhere near his father.

At a place where three roads meet, not far from Thebes, Oedipus runs into an old man with guards driving a wagon in a very aggressive way. The man is rude and hostile, and orders Oedipus to get off the road. He refuses to comply, so the old man starts to beat him with a club. Oedipus, in a state of distress, becomes enraged and kills the old man and two of his guards. When Oedipus arrives in Thebes, he finds the place is being terrorised by a monster, a hybrid creature with the head of a woman and the body of a winged lioness, who destroys all those who cannot answer her riddle. Oedipus answers the riddle correctly, and is given the kingdom of Thebes in return. He is also given the hand of the queen, who has been recently widowed.

Years pass, and Oedipus and Jocasta have four children. Then a terrible plague begins in Thebes, a disease (thought to be caused by sin) that kills animals, crops and children. Oedipus sends his brother-in-law to consult the Oracle, who tells him that the plague has been caused by the unpunished murder of King Laius.

Oedipus turns for help to the prophet Tiresias, who tells him he is the killer, and that he has also perpetrated other terrible crimes. Oedipus is furious, and nearly has Tiresias and his brother-in-law killed. Jocasta soothes him by telling him that the Oracle speaks nonsense – she herself was told by the Oracle that their son would kill her husband, and their son had died as a baby – and that her husband had been killed by robbers at a place where three roads meet. Oedipus remembers killing a man at such a place. Jocasta says there is a witness to the killing – a man who escaped from the robbers. At the same time as the witness is sent for, a messenger arrives from Corinth to tell Oedipus that Polybus, the man he believes to be his father, is dead, and that he is now the King of Corinth. Oedipus says he can never go back, as the Oracle told him he would end up making love to his mother. 'But she is not your mother,' the messenger replied, revealing to Oedipus that he was given to Polybus as a baby. Jocasta suddenly knows the awful truth.

The slave who witnessed the murder of Laius turns out to be the same man who gave the baby Oedipus to his friend. Oedipus realises his true identity, and goes to find Jocasta. She has hanged herself. Oedipus takes the shoulder pins from her dress and blinds himself. For the second and final time, he is taken out on the mountain to die.

Freud's description of the infant wishing to rid himself of the parent of the same sex so that he can marry his mother seemed to fit exactly with the material dealt with in the Greek myth. That's how he came to call it the 'Oedipus complex'. After all, the child has no idea of adult sexual relationships – the child's sexuality is not geared towards sexual intercourse, but rather towards pleasurable feelings, such as that produced by eating an ice cream. The child sees no reason why he can't be perfectly happy with his mum, living on the seashore, making sandcastles. He is in a state of ecstasy in her arms, he loves her beyond all others, he loves the way she smells, feels and looks – he loves the way she loves him. The only problem is that Dad doesn't seem too happy about the amount of time Mum spends with her little boy, and keeps trying to take her away from him. As Freud says in his *Introductory Lectures on Psychoanalysis*:

> There is no need to feel surprised, therefore, if in a large number of people, dreams disclose their wish to get rid of the parent of the same sex ... While he is still a small child, a son will already begin to develop a special affection for his mother, whom he regards as belonging to him; he begins to feel his father as a rival who disputes his sole possession.

Barriers

Freud speaks of the barriers that gradually form into rigid taboos as we mature – the barrier of species (the gulf between men and animals); the barrier against incest (seeking sexual satisfaction from near blood-relatives); the barrier against members of the same sex.

> None of these barriers existed from the beginning. Small children are free from them. They recognise no frightful gulf between human beings and animals; the arrogance with which human beings separate themselves from animals does not emerge until later. To begin with, children exhibit no disgust at excreta but acquire this slowly under the pressure of education; they attach no special importance to the

distinction between the sexes … they direct their first sexual
lusts and their curiosity to those who are nearest and dearest
to them – parents, brothers and sisters, nurses.

Of course it should be stated at this point that Freud was in no way
saying that these first sexual feelings in children should be taken as
provocation or seduction in adult terms. He rather saw it as an
undeniable fact that the boy child has the parent of the opposite sex –
his first love – right there by the side of his cradle from the very
beginning. Christiane Olivier, in her book *Jocasta's Children*, speaks of
the compelling 'first-love' situation between mothers and boys in the
following terms:

Is there a man, is there a son anywhere who can say that he
has really got rid of his mother? Oh – he'll have left her all
right, but how far did he get? Left her for whom? Is there a
mother anywhere who could say that she has given up her
son, even when she's 80? He is still 'the one' … the bond that
is woven between mother and son in infancy binds them
together forever. When a woman marries, she can only ever
marry another woman's son.

Olivier sees the growing boy as being engaged in a desperate struggle
to break free of his mother's fondness for him. We know about
Oedipus, she says, but Jocasta – what of her? She was happily married
to her son, as he was to her. 'The woman has unconscious difficulties
about giving up the only male she has ever been able to keep close by
her; she whose father let her down, and whose husband is more often
away than at home.'

The result seems to be, says Olivier, that men are continually trying
to keep women at a distance in their adult life, holding them at bay,
resisting the suffocating closeness they experienced with the love-
hungry mother.

For the man, what is born here is the tenderest of all loves followed by the most long-drawn out of wars. From this, the man emerges showing signs of distrust, silence, misogyny; in a word all the things women reproach men with.

Ryan's story

The T-shirts that have become fashionable in the last few years, bearing slogans like 'Boys Lie' or 'Boys Cheat', give voice to a prevailing mistrust of men. Julie Matthews' song 'The Thorn upon the Rose' (performed so hauntingly by the Irish singer Mary Black) expresses the very familiar, age-old feeling – the need and longing of the woman versus the uncaring flight of the man:

Its taste was sweet like summer wine,
The heart that beats in double time.
So he waltzed right in and bowled you over
And you're still reeling from the feeling when he's gone.
The door is closed, the lock is turned,
And all the memories and letters have been burned –
So when you pick the handsome flower
Don't forget the thorn upon the rose!
Its cut is deep and the scar lasts forever:
It follows love wherever love goes.

Although the dreadful hurt described in this song is often seen to be caused by a deliberate, or at best negligent, cruelty on the part of men, the truth may be somewhat different. In the consulting room, men often express feelings of fear, inadequacy and guilt. Ryan, at 33, finds intimacy hard to bear. His mother was just 19 when he and his twin sister were born. Ryan's dad was hardly ever at home – at 23, his main concern was to be a good provider for his growing family and young wife. He worked every hour God sent. When he was at home, he was so tired that he was irritable and scarcely able to communicate. Ryan can't recall any time that his father 'just played' with him and his sister. What he can recall, however, is that he was very aware of his parents' sexual relationship. He remembers lying awake and hearing them moaning and crying out, hearing the bed creak repeatedly. He remembers his mother getting into bed with him 'for a cuddle' when she passed his bedroom on the way to the toilet – he thinks now this must have been straight after she had been making love with his dad – she was naked. He remembers the feel of her silky body and how lovely it was. He remembers the agony of her leaving him after a few tantalising minutes. He remembers how fat she suddenly looked to him as he watched her naked body walking away.

Ryan, now an adult man, finds it almost impossible to feel accepting of women. He is constantly critical of them, his focus especially on their weight. He is acutely sensitive to the reactions of other men to his current girlfriend. In therapy he tells me about his suffering – how much he would like a satisfying long-term relationship. He knows how much he sabotages this wish by the extremity of his quest for perfection. He finds sexual intimacy with women an on-going challenge – he experiences a great ambivalence. His body wants to be close and fulfilled, but his feelings reject the act of sex – he experiences it as being crushed and oppressed – owned, possessed, as if the woman were using him and even abusing him. After sex, he feels agonised and empty, often compelled to end the relationship there and then. D.H. Lawrence, writing eighty years ago, describes this feeling perfectly in his great work *Women in Love*:

> On the whole, he hated sex, it was such a limitation. It was sex that turned a man into a broken half of a couple, the woman into the other broken half. And he wanted to be single in himself, the woman single in herself. He wanted sex to revert to the level of other appetites, to be regarded as a functional process, not as a fulfilment … He wanted so much to be free, not under the compulsion of any need for

unification, or tortured by unsatisfied desires … The merging, the clutching, the mingling of love had become madly abhorrent to him … it seemed to him, woman was always so horrible and clutching, she had such a lust for possession, a greed of self-importance in love.

Confusing messages

The experience many men seem to have of being mothered is an alternating and confusing sense of being pulled towards and pushed away from this crucial woman. Sometimes she picks them up when they don't want to be picked up, when they want to run free; sometimes she puts them down when they long to cling to her and feel her softness and warmth. Ryan's experience was exaggerated by having a little female opponent for his mother's love. His twin was seen as a quiet and 'good' child – he was seen as a 'naughty' tearaway who was always running off and getting lost. As they grew from children to teenagers, Ryan had two women he loved and hated – his mother and his sister – two women he longed for but couldn't have, two women who could command the adoration and attention of his often-absent father. Post puberty, Ryan remembers the clouds of sweet perfume in the bathroom, the pretty, frilly clothes and underwear, the tantalising flashes of bare flesh he would see through open doors. There seemed to be an unspoken understanding, a bond, between his mother and his sister that was not available to him. They seemed to tease him, flirt with him and then send him away. As Lawrence puts it:

> He has come from an unattainable idyll with one woman – his mother. What he is looking for is an idyll – attainable now – with another woman – one who is, this time, allowed.

Closeness and distance

As the boy grows into a man, the breach widens. At some level, which is perhaps inaccessible to his conscious thoughts, he remembers the intensity of that early relationship between his adored baby-self and his adoring mother. At some stage he endures the undeniable reality that the woman he loves so fervently belongs to another man – a man to whom he is also intimately connected – his father. One response to this wound can be to suppress all talk of loving a woman. From the little boy who tells his mum over and over how much he loves her, how she is 'the best mum in the whole world', the little boy who dreams that one day he will marry her and be with her forever, comes the young man who seems to despise the girls around him.

The feeling language of love is a frightening area for men to re-enter when it has been suppressed and repressed by the pain of the forced distance he must keep from his mother – and in Ryan's case, from his sister too. All too often it vanishes entirely, leaving women feeling neglected and unloved. In so many of the couples I see for counselling, the complaint voiced by the woman centres around her partner's lack of response, lack of communication – coldness, withholding. He seems to prefer to do almost anything with his male friends than to be with her. Christiane Olivier writes in *Jocasta's Children*:

> In the typical case, the man, in the wake of the Oedipal collision which is the boy's lot, has had to put behind him loving feelings, tears, other signs of emotion – all of them marks of weakness – to be associated with women. And with that, he cuts off a whole dimension of love – the dimension of language. Rare indeed is the man who is a talkative lover.

Older woman, younger man

How can a woman trust a boy's love, when the boy, we must assume, has been irrevocably wounded by another woman, the most important woman of all? In their fascinating study of older women and younger men, *Older Women/Younger Men: New Options for Love and Romance*, Felicia Brings and Susan Winter spoke to two hundred couples in which the women were at least ten years older than the men. Susan is an exceptionally beautiful and talented woman – a professional communicator and an inspirational speaker, who models for the famous Chaos Comics action figure Lady Death. She obviously has a lot of choice in her selection of a partner. She prefers relationships with younger men. Here is what she told me about her view of 'a boy's love':

> Experience can jade us, and make us bitter and shut down emotionally. A boy's love is still close to the pure state. It is unguarded. It is raw and uncensored. It lacks self-consciousness and editing. It doesn't come with the baggage of the many former hurts. There is a spontaneity about youthful love – it is still idealistic and natural. Younger men have a reasonably clean slate, and are much more apt to enter into a relationship with a 'let's see' attitude rather than a 'she'd better not' attitude. Because on some levels they are not yet fully formed, they are still open to listening and evaluating the feelings and activities they experience.

In the last twenty years there has been a huge increase in general knowledge about psychological ideas. Best-selling books such as *Men Are from Mars, Women Are from Venus* by John Gray, *Emotional Intelligence* by Daniel Goleman, and Stephanie Dowrick's wonderful mix of Buddhist teaching and psychotherapeutic ideas *Forgiveness and Other Acts of Love* have been key players in the growth in understanding we have gained of ourselves and others. Susan Winter sees this understanding manifested in younger rather than older men:

> The openness of youth allows for new information and new attitudes. Younger generations are schooled in pop psychology. Current songs depict narratives using such terms as 'dysfunctional' and 'co-dependent'. There is much more known and appreciated about the dynamics of healthy relationships. When involved with a younger man who has an awareness of this current knowledge, an older woman has an established rapport of emotional language that is heard. The communication of feelings can be more easily articulated and understood.

The strong and silent type

The difficulty in communicating with their partners often seems the crucial issue to many of the women I see for therapy. The frustration and anger generated by 'stonewalling' (withdrawal and angry silence) seems to be most often felt by women in response to men who will not or cannot express their ambivalent feelings. Many men prefer to remove themselves from a potentially threatening or deeply confusing interchange. Professor of Linguistics Dr Deborah Tannen, in her book *That's Not What I Meant!*, explains how she sees the conversational style of men and women as hugely different. She describes the stereotype of the 'strong silent type' by referring to the actor Henry Fonda:

> Jack Kroll, writing about Henry Fonda on the occasion of his death, used the phrases 'quiet power', 'abashed silences', 'combustible catatonia' and 'sense of power held in check' ... the resulting silence was effective on stage, but devastating to his family. The image of the silent father is common and is

often the model for the lover or the husband. But what attracts us can become the flypaper to which we are unhappily stuck. Nancy Schoenberger begins a poem with the lines: 'It was your silence that hooked me/ So like my father's.' Adrienne Rich refers in a poem to 'the husband who is frustratingly mute'. Despite the initial attraction of such quintessentially male silence, it may begin to feel, to a woman in a long-term relationship, like a brick wall against which she is banging her head.

The Dad factor

Just as relevant to women as to men, the Oedipus myth seems to suggest that we cannot escape our powerful attraction to the parent of the opposite sex. As mothers to our daughters, we come from a position of deprivation – like giving food away when we are starving to death. In so many cultures, the son is prized, the daughter despised. Jocasta's love affair is with her son. Statistics point to the fact that boys are breast-fed longer than girls. The empty feeling so many women complain about seems to originate in the lack of desire felt for them by their mothers. The bitter, intense and rivalrous relationships that emerge between mother and adolescent daughter are all too often enacted under the absent father's roof – he provides for the main players in the drama, but is very rarely on the stage himself. Susan Winter told me:

My father was the centre of my life, and all things good and wonderful. He was intelligent, powerful, yet humble, authentic and successful. He ran an oil company, and was an incredible human being. He wanted to be a doctor, so he got a chemistry degree. Before his senior year, he got a summer job cleaning oil tanks. By the end of that summer he was working inside the office. By 34, he was president of that same company.

Although Susan grew up with an adoring father in a materially privileged and seemingly loving home, her relationship with her mother was painful and confusing:

> During my years growing up at home, there were constant battles between my Mother and myself. As a child I didn't understand it and assumed she just didn't love me. As I got older, it became clear that her jealousy and rage were fuelled by perceiving me as 'the other woman'. I didn't see any competition. I was the child, she was the wife. I just wanted a mommy I could love and trust, but she was violent and unpredictable. I never knew whether I'd be greeted with a slap or a hug. I totally withdrew from her emotionally. My need for my Father grew as I feared and mistrusted my Mother. He was my world – the only one I trusted and loved. Neither my Father nor I understood the disease of alcoholism at the time. Being isolated from other children and an only child, I didn't have anyone to turn to but my Father. This intensified the circle of jealousy, rage and violence. It's taken my Father's death, years of therapy and inner work to retrieve my mommy – she has 30 years of sobriety, and I finally have a Mother.

Although Susan's life is very much the way she wants it to be now, she is fully aware of the deep impact that her early relationships with the two key people in her life still has on her current relationships with men. She puts it eloquently:

> As long as Daddy was perfect, there was no room for another man. Oddly enough it was my much younger boyfriend who helped me to see that I had put my father on a pedestal.

'Hated Bad Mommy' and 'Saintly Perfect Daddy' = concrete thinking – my black and white childhood perceptions. Only when I recognized the full dimension of both parents was I free to enter a deeper and more realistic view of loving relationships with men. And only then was I able to incorporate the abandoned female aspects I discarded from my Mother.

Kohut and idealisation

Susan's description echoes Kohut's belief that children have a pressing need to idealise one or both parents, and keep them good. Kohut saw the self of the child as a tiny seed, needing food and water and sunlight to grow into a strong and healthy plant. In the child's case, as well as the physical requirements needed for optimal health, vital nutrients for emotional well-being are found in the responses and modelling provided by parents. Kohut believed that, in order to develop a strong and healthy sense of self, children have two crucial needs. The first is the need to be mirrored – in other words to be admired for their achievements and special gifts; to be encouraged and validated. This is not at all the same as being pressured to achieve results on behalf of the parent; rather it is a confirmation of the child's uniqueness and difference from the parent. The second is the need to idealise the parent. Kohut believed this need to be paramount to the development of confidence and self-soothing in the child, and that if it is not met, it can result in agonising anxiety and ambivalence.

At pre-puberty and puberty, children need to take in values and meaning from their parents and teachers, and need to have modelled for them decency, self-respect and compassion for others. If for some reason the parent is deeply flawed and displays unpredictable, alcoholic or addictive behaviour, or the parent is seriously ill or dies, the growing self of the child can be permanently damaged in the area of control and self-soothing. Obsessional or compulsive symptoms can develop in a frantic attempt to grab control of a chaotic and dangerous internal situation. Crayton Rowe and David MacIsaac, writing about Kohut's theories in *Empathic Attunement*, make the following observation:

> The despair and depression that often follow severe disappointment during adolescence – such as disillusionment with an idealized figure – is well-known. Hope for the future and life itself can be diminished. It is also well-known that suicides have occurred when teenage idols have died. Similarly, disappointments leading to despair at the ending of romantic relationships have resulted in many tragic adolescent suicides. Great numbers of teenagers have turned to peer groups, cults, drugs and sexual promiscuity out of deep disappointment with parental figures – disappointment that can be generalized to include disillusionment with the norms of society or with the political system.

Susan, dreadfully disillusioned with her mother in adolescence, turned to her father for all her idealising needs – this is why she describes discarding 'the abandoned female aspects of Mother'. Instead of modelling herself on her mother, she looked to her father to provide a model for life. She describes the process perfectly:

> I was able to envision myself in his eyes. I felt strong, capable, smart, beautiful, talented and respected. If I hadn't had his love to balance me, I wouldn't have been able to survive the rest of it. I created my template of what love looks like from watching him. He was wise, open-minded and non-judgemental. He looked at the soul of a person … he made people smile, because we all felt good about ourselves in his presence …

Although Susan was deeply disillusioned by her mother, she was able to idealise her father, and this provided her with the inner strength to find the values of love, compassion and respect that have been so important to her as an adult.

Love and loss

Susan told me of the terrible impact of seeing her father have a heart attack when she was nine:

> We were all in the kitchen. It was dinner time. Suddenly my Dad collapsed, grabbing at his heart. He turned grey. He was trying to speak – my Mother was hysterical. I remember her screaming at me to go upstairs to my room. I was frightened. And furious at my Mother for sending me out of the room. I wouldn't leave the staircase. I wanted to help – I kept screaming 'Daddy! Daddy!'

In that moment, Susan lost the strong, infallible father of her early childhood. At the tender age of nine years old (when she recalled it first, she thought she had been only five, she felt so small and useless; it was later that she realised she must have been nine), Susan was no longer able to imagine her father as invulnerable – instead she had to face his impending death in an agonising and confusing way. Not knowing if he would live or die at that moment, she was heartbroken that she couldn't help him. From that moment, she knew she had to protect him, even from her own pain. 'One effect of his heart attack was the "don't tell" rule. When my mother and I would fight, she'd manipulate me into silence with the "If you tell your father we fought, you'll give him another heart attack".'

Her father died after open heart surgery when Susan was 34 years old. It was an exceptionally traumatic parting. Yet inside Susan, her father stayed alive. From babyhood she had observed his care and nurturing of others, and she is aware that this is what she has offered to others in the way that he offered it to her:

> Looking after men is the result of taking on my Father's role in relationships. Since he was my only example of love, I did what he did. I've nurtured, supported, built up and helped men in each and every relationship. In my last relationship, I constantly heard my inner self say: 'I don't want to be the Daddy any more – I want a man to nurture and help me.'

From the depth of her self-knowledge and experience of life and love, Susan has understood that she has been offering to her younger lovers precisely those qualities for which she is yearning.

The need for love

Psychoanalyst Richard O'Neill Dean, in his paper 'Falling in (to the need for) Love', says the following:

> When we fall in love, our subjective experience is that we feel something for the other, that we have something to give the other. In fact we are driven by unrecognised need. We have not fallen in love – we have fallen in (to the need for) love.

Richard talks of this need as a leftover longing for a mother-baby merging:

> Falling in love is experienced as fated, god-given – a sort of 'all history leads to this moment' feeling. There is intense excitement and an absolute certainty. The other is experienced as special, ideal and wonderful. Life cannot be lived without contact with this other. There is a tender wish to give tokens of affection. I compare these qualities to the merged relationship between mother and infant. In this 'has-to-be' timelessness, there is nothing else of importance.

> Excitements and intimacies are maximal. The fundamental
> wish to be the object of desire of the other is realised.

In our intimate relationships we are hoping to find a repeat of that unique, exciting and all-consuming feeling that we once knew with the loved parent. So often this hope is dashed by the disappointment we experience in our quest for the ideal other. Susan is acutely aware of the legacy with which she is living:

> We hear a lot about the women who can't trust men because
> of their abusive or emotionally bereft Fathers, but there's a
> double-edged sword with the fabulous Father. He's set the bar
> quite high. I find myself saying no to most men I meet, and
> yes to only a very select few. There can be years in between
> relationships for me, while many women I know are constantly
> involved. The good news is that at least I like my own
> company while I sit out the dance.

To trust each other in our intimate relationships is perhaps to come to terms with the unrealistic expectations we are holding close to our hearts, the memories of the golden times. In these 400- year-old lines, Henry Vaughan expresses our longing poignantly in his poem 'The Retreat':

> Happy those early days, when I
> Shined in my angel-infancy!

Trusting a boy's love – or a girl's – we must reconcile ourselves to the loss of those shining days. Richard O'Neill Dean puts it succinctly: 'Life is not perfect. Relationship is not perfect. The partner is not perfect. We must make friends with frustration.'

Chapter 6

Men in Love

In the summer of 1974, I was working as a volunteer on a kibbutz near Galilee. Every Saturday night a film would be shown on a rickety old screen rigged up at the end of the dining room. The ceiling of this room rolled back like a blind, and when the sun had gone down the stars were like millions of tiny lamps in the black sky above us. There were about fifty volunteers from all over the world – in particular from the UK, Europe, Australia, the US and Canada – and about three hundred kibbutzniks who lived in what amounted to a small village dedicated to farming and exporting the beautiful fruit for which the kibbutz was famous. On this particular night, the film that had been chosen was Ken Russell's brilliant adaptation of D.H. Lawrence's *Women in Love*.

A strange experience in the heat of the Mediterranean night – to be watching the dark satanic mills of Yorkshire and the snowfields of the Swiss Alps, and the very English actors, Glenda Jackson, Alan Bates, Oliver Reed, Eleanor Bron – but not nearly as strange as the sudden evacuation of the dining room by almost all of the kibbutzniks when a certain scene began to play out. Readers familiar with the movie will remember the famous naked wrestling scene, when Gerald (Oliver Reed in his young and glorious days) and Rupert (Alan Bates) strip and engage in a bout of fighting in front of a blazing log fire in the drawing room of an English country home.

Although this is a highly charged scene, full of sexual tension, neither of the men is portrayed as homosexual. They are both involved with female partners – the women in love. It was, I suppose, a shocking scene for some – typical Ken Russell, people might say. He was a director known for heady, sexually explicit imagery. I had seen the film previously in England, and had felt a collective intake of breath as this scene played out. But nothing prepared me for the mass walk-out that happened so spontaneously this night. There was an audible ripple of protest, then suddenly only we volunteers were left in the open dining room, crickets chirping in the dark night outside, a cat sauntering over the top of the screen. We looked at each other in amazement and laughed a little, before the movie re-engaged us.

At that time, kibbutzim in Israel were renowned for 'soldier-making'. If a man and woman living on a kibbutz managed to produce five children, they were rewarded with a car. A population under constant threat, Israel was intent on becoming strong and numerous. My tentative enquiries about the walk-out resulted in the information that homosexuality was seen as a betrayal of the state; a decadent behaviour perpetrated by Arabs; an embarrassment; a violation. It was quite simple: two men taking off their clothes equalled homosexuality. I remember the sadness I felt, the feeling that there had been some ghastly mistake, a misunderstanding. Later, arriving back home, I turned again to Lawrence's extraordinary tribute to the complexity of our sexuality. Here is what he writes in the book *Women in Love* about the truth of that naked fight between the two men:

> So the two men entwined and wrestled with each other,
> working nearer and nearer. Both were white and clear, but
> Gerald flushed smart red where he was touched, and Birkin
> remained white and tense. He seemed to penetrate into
> Gerald's more solid, more diffuse bulk, to interfuse his body
> through the body of the other, as if to bring it subtly into
> subjection, always seizing with some rapid necromantic
> foreknowledge every motion of the other flesh, converting

and counteracting it, playing on the limbs and trunk of Gerald like some hard wind. It was as if Birkin's whole physical intelligence interpenetrated into Gerald's body, as if his fine, sublimated energy entered into the flesh of the fuller man, like some potency, casting a fine net, a prison, through the muscles into the very depths of Gerald's physical being.

The description of the physical, naked contact between the two men, the repetition of words like 'penetrate' and the sheer intensity of the passage have a disturbing impact on the reader. Yet it represents a hymn of triumphant praise to the contact between two human beings who are involved with each other on many levels. At one stage, when the sparring is done and the two men are lying exhausted on the carpet, Birkin attempts to sit up, putting out his hand to steady himself: 'It touched the hand of Gerald, that was lying out on the floor. And Gerald's hand closed warm and sudden over Birkin's, they remained exhausted and breathless, the one hand clasped closely over the other.'

Homophobia

The unease and anxiety many people feel when they are confronted by imagery that implies same-sex desire can become fear and loathing if self-knowledge is absent. These are the roots of homophobia. For the kibbutzniks, with their strong cultural imperative to bring children into the world, it was too much to contemplate that two men might strip off and allow themselves naked body contact with each other and might then lie exhausted and holding hands. As Freud writes in *Introductory Lectures on Psychoanalysis*:

> We describe a sexual activity as perverse if it has given up the aim of reproduction and pursues the attainment of pleasure as

an aim independent of it … the breach and turning point in
the development of sexual life lies in its becoming
subordinate to the purposes of reproduction.

It seems important to emphasise that when Freud uses the word
'perverse', he is talking about a differing from the 'normal' acceptance
of prohibitions and taboos – barriers constructed by the society in
which we live, for example the barrier against incest. Yet Freud asserts:
'Psychoanalytic research has shown, unmistakably, that the choice of
an incestuous love object is the first and invariable one and that it is
not until later that resistance to it sets in.' Resistance occurs when the
child struggles to adapt to societal pressures and expectations, to
renounce the instinctive nature of childhood, and instead, feels
compelled to accept the rules of the grown-up world.

Julian and Tim

Julian is a psychotherapist who works with both gay and straight
clients. He is in his late fifties. He has given much time and
consideration to the struggle for identity experienced by many gay
men:

> I don't like calling myself gay any more – it's restrictive,
> categorising, diagnosing. Whereas 'queer' for me means
> being free to explore. My search has been a complicated one.
> I've been searching for my sexuality and my heredity with my
> father.

Men's relationships with men begin with the father. Julian wonders
what men can do with that love, and returns again to the ideas
contained in the myth of Oedipus and the murder of father to clear the
path towards mother:

> We either kill our fathers in order to be free to love, or

sexualise the relationship and then transfer that onto other men. There's a strong historical tradition of men learning to be men by being in a sexual relationship with older men. There are tribes whose rites of passage for young men involve ingesting the sperm of older men, so that they can drink in the strength and courage and become men in their turn.

Frank Browning, in his work *A Queer Geography*, writes of the Sambian people of New Guinea:

> The Sambia men believe that boys cannot become men unless they suck out male essence – semen – and fill up their semen organ through which they become strong. In their understanding of biology, males cannot generate their own semen. They must instead get it from older men, and then once having it, they can pass it on.

This account seems relevant to Julian's memories of a very intense relationship with a younger man. At the time, Julian was in his forties and living in London, training to be a psychotherapist. Julian lived in an attic room in a typical London street, the house backing onto a garden and then the back of another street. Every night, he would watch a boy in a house on the other street. The boy would dance at his window at night. Sometimes he would dance with a cloak, and sometimes he would dance naked – it was very erotic and enticing:

> I was captivated by it. I used to watch and wait for him. It became quite compulsive in a way, and I never knew if he knew that I could see him. So one night, I lit a candle and put it in my window, and waited. The next night, he lit a candle. So I lit two candles, and then he lit two candles. And so, we developed this communication – he was very seductive. And one night, I very obviously put my coat on, and turned on the

lights so it showed I was going down the stairs, and went out.
I went past his house, and he came out with his coat on. And
we walked along together and started a conversation.

Julian found out that his mysterious friend was 18 and that his name
was Tim. He learned about Tim's family, that his mother had left when
he was quite young and that Tim lived with his father and brother.
They talked of Tim's feelings about being gay. From that night on,
Julian and Tim began a relationship. Julian would come home from his
classes and as soon as the light went on in his room, Tim would come
round:

> It was very tender – an initiation of a kind – it was wholesome,
> and good – it was all right. And then one day, he didn't come
> round, and the blinds were down in his room. It stayed like
> that, and I went round in the end and left a note for him, but
> he still didn't come back. Time passed by, and I stopped
> looking out of the window – occasionally I'd see moments of
> him, but there was no communication. And then one day I
> bumped into him in the street. I asked him what happened – I
> said I thought we loved each other. He said, 'Yes we do, but
> it's impossible.' I think maybe his father found out, or maybe
> he got scared.

Some time later, Tim's brother stopped Julian in the street. 'I know who
you are!' he said. Julian felt suddenly shamed, and accused, 'like a
dirty old man', although he knew this was not how things had been.
He was hurt, too, by what felt like a sudden dismissal. He still thinks
about the relationship with Tim:

> The pain is not knowing what Tim made of it. I think it was a
> respectful, warm, loving encounter and I think he would have
> thought that – I know he would have thought that. I feel sad

he had to run away like that. And now when I think about it, I think it is so easy for a son to hurt a father, and the father somehow is not allowed to acknowledge that. And it's about power too – power bouncing backwards and forwards like ping-pong. And I often think of that. I gave Tim a candlestick, I remember, which seemed significant, as we met through candles. I often wonder if he's still got it. And he gave me a CD of his favourite film. I still play it sometimes.

Julian's memories of this man–boy relationship evoke many questions about the relationship of the son to the father:

And I wonder – is the gay son created by the absent father? Does the father recognise something and then retreat or does the son recognise something and then the father's not there? And always in relationships there are those two sides.

Duncan

For Duncan, too, the impact of his father's emotional absence has taken its toll on his life. Duncan is a 37-year-old gay man who works as an administrator for a major London theatre. He is articulate, honest, generous and warm. For the last three years he has lived in a monogamous relationship with Andrew. He ascribes the success of this relationship to the fact that he has been able, for the first time, to love himself. 'Not in an arrogant way – just accepting myself and able to appreciate myself without criticism or judgement.'

It hadn't always been like this for Duncan. He described to me the restless ten years of searching and longing, during which he had felt so desperate at times he had resorted to taking cocaine and ecstasy every weekend to alter his mood and to anaesthetise the pain: '… doing what was necessary to gain approval and fit in with the scene – whatever it took to make me feel high, sexy and attractive – looking back, it all seems so exhausting'.

Duncan is aware that the poor self-image and low self-esteem he experienced for so many years were largely the result of his unhappy schooldays and the difficult relationship he had with his father, who was mostly absent during his childhood, leaving him enmeshed in a smothering relationship with his mother. As he got older, Duncan realised his dad had a problem with alcohol:

> By late afternoon, on most days, he had drunk too much alcohol and it was impossible for us to have any kind of satisfactory or meaningful conversation. During my teenage years, he was, on many occasions, a rude, aggressive, unsupportive and extremely critical bully. By the time I reached the age of 16, our relationship had completely disintegrated.

Duncan told me that it was around the age of 12 that he began to realise he was 'different'. It was the late 1970s, and he lived in a small village in the south of England. There was no-one he felt he could talk to – his experience was of terrified isolation. Duncan was never 'overtly effeminate', but sensitive and gentle, not interested in sports, and obviously unable to discuss the teenage 'petting sessions' which the other boys avidly recounted to each other. He knew he was sexually attracted to other boys, and it didn't take long for the name-calling to start.

> As I was neither strong nor aggressive, I was an easy target for verbal and physical abuse. My feelings of isolation grew into feelings of shame and sadness. I had desperately low self-esteem and was living in a constant state of fear. Ask any child who has been humiliated and bullied – they will easily recall the sleepless nights and nightmare mornings, the knotted stomach and the endless days.

Duncan's family moved nearer to London when he was 15. He hoped beyond hope that things might improve, that he could have a new beginning. He wanted so much to belong, to feel accepted. But the bullying in his new school was even more vicious, and he became the target of six boys who regularly subjected him to violent abuse. On one occasion he was attacked by the boys, dragged to the floor and punched and kicked several times. He was then punished for being involved in what the headmaster called 'over-enthusiastic rough and tumble'. The violent episode was one of many – Duncan felt traumatised, scared and alone, with very little sense of self-love and self-worth. As an adult, he found himself bouncing from one bad relationship to another:

> Lack of self-belief would mean that on the occasions when I would meet a genuine, honest and caring guy who also happened to look gorgeous, I would be thinking – why does he fancy me? If he treated me with respect and love, I would begin to feel uncomfortable and any sexual interest I had for him would just disappear.

Duncan went on to describe the obsession with appearance that he sees as predominant in the gay community:

> The vast majority of the gay papers and magazines are filled with pictures of beautiful, young, healthy boys who are often semi-naked. The adverts and articles are usually focused on trips to the gym, what to wear and how to get more sex – I don't think I ever trusted a boy's love, because I never felt any love for myself. I didn't feel handsome enough, smart enough or good enough. I didn't have the faintest idea of how to love myself. I was always waiting for someone to appear who would make me feel whole, happy and safe. Trusting someone was such a frightening thing to do.

Duncan also takes account of the agonising toll taken on his life by the homophobia endemic in the society in which he grew up:

> It's an old cliche, but you can never love anybody else until you learn to love yourself. This is true of all of us – male, female, gay and straight. However, for many, many gay people, lack of self-love is an acute problem. Homophobia, lack of support from family, friends and society, can result in severe and longlasting psychological problems.

Sodom and Gomorrah

Professor Byrne Fone, in his illuminating and fascinating work *Homophobia: A History*, traces homophobia back to the Old Testament. He quotes from the Book of Genesis, which tells the story of the people of Sodom and Gomorrah. The term 'sodomite' has become synonymous with men who practise same-sex intercourse, and it has been generally believed that the terrible crimes of the people of Sodom – unspeakable and horrific in a vague and nightmarish kind of way – centred around orgies and blasphemy. God sent two angels to the city to find out what was going on. It seems, as Professor Fone points out, that the whole idea that the people of Sodom were homosexuals hinges on two verses from Genesis 19. The angels have been invited into Lot's house to eat and rest, while the men of Sodom gather outside Lot's house:

> And they called unto Lot, and said unto him: 'Where are the men which came in to thee this night. Bring them out to us that we may know them.'
> And Lot went out at the door unto them, and shut the door after him, and said
> 'I pray you, brethren, do not so wickedly.'

Professor Fone points out that the whole case rests on the verb 'to know':

> The Sodomites' demand to 'know' the angels is interpreted as the cause of their devastating punishment. In the Hebrew text, the verb is 'yadha'. 'Yadha' appears some nine hundred times in the Old Testament, and almost always it means 'to become acquainted with'. In a handful of cases however, 'yadha' can also be understood, perhaps euphemistically, to imply sexual activity with someone.

Sodom was indeed destroyed in a catastrophe – Professor Fone tells us that a disaster did occur in the Cities of the Plain near the Dead Sea. It is generally believed by archaeologists that a huge earthquake may have ignited subterranean gases, resulting in a terrifying series of explosions and fires. However, the idea that this disaster was visited on the area because of the practice of homosexuality seems to rest on what Professor Fone calls 'a tragic misunderstanding'. He goes on to trace the wildfire spread of the accusation of sodomy, which became one and the same as heresy, and entire populations were found guilty of this sin and punished accordingly. So the laws against homosexuality were set in stone, and that stone was used as a weapon of torture and murder against all those who were seen as the enemies of Christianity: 'A weapon effective against political enemies, the charge of sodomy could also be employed against entire peoples and systems of belief.'

During the Crusades, Muslim and Jewish 'infidels' were believed to be rampantly homosexual, and the punishment for their crimes was to be buried alive.

Varieties of punishment for same-sex relationships have continued to be meted out – only sixty-five years ago, Hitler attempted to wipe out homosexuals in his quest to establish the Master Race. Many males from all nations were persecuted, tortured and executed. Hitler even searched his own men for signs of homosexuality, and sent any suspects to concentration camps. Homosexual inmates in the camps were forced to wear pink triangles, and were subjected to countless intense and painful humiliations before dying in the gas ovens. Fifteen thousand homosexuals died during the Holocaust.

Professor Fone's statistics of current attitudes show how prevalent the hatred of difference remains:

> In 1997, 44% of Americans surveyed believed that homosexual relations between consenting adults should not be legal; of those who called themselves Christians, 69% believed this. In 1998, though 84% of the sample were willing to extend equal rights in the workplace to homosexuals, 64% of Christians were not. Also, in 1998, 54% of those surveyed still believed homosexuality to be 'a sin', and even more – 59% – believed it to be morally wrong.

Self-respect

With the knowledge that homosexuality has continued for so many centuries to be deemed a crime, that the most appalling punishments have been dealt out to men who prefer relationships with other men and that homophobia flourishes in the 'civilised world', perpetuating hatred and discrimination, how can a gay man begin to respect and trust himself?

Despite his horrible encounters with homophobic bullying and the discrimination he has so often encountered, Duncan has begun to believe in himself, and for the first time in his life he trusts the love of another man:

> I believe that we teach others how to treat us. If we have love and respect for ourselves and others, this will be visible in our behaviour. As a result, people will be unlikely to mistreat and

abuse us. If they do, then we will have the strength and the ability to move away from destructive people and situations. At the time I met Andrew, I no longer needed other people's approval and acceptance in order for me to live my life. I had my own acceptance and approval, and this is far more powerful. It is also permanent. Because of this I am able to trust his love without worrying and fearing that it may be taken away. No-one can take away the love I now have for myself.

Chapter 7

A Whore's Oath

What does the word 'whore' mean? It appears to have Indo-European roots. One derivative of the original root 'ka', meaning to like or to desire, has given us words like 'charity', 'cherish' and 'caress'. The Italian word 'caro', meaning dear, comes from this root, as does the Sanskrit word for love, 'kama'. The other derivative, 'horaz', a common Germanic word, also meant 'one who desires', or sometimes 'adulterer', and the feminine of this became 'horon', the ancestor of the modern English word 'whore'. Webster's Revised and Unabridged Dictionary gives three meanings (the first two refer to the verb, the third to the noun):

1. To have unlawful sexual intercourse; to practice lewdness
2. To worship false and impure gods
3. A woman who engages in sexual intercourse for money.

The word's gradual slide, from its sense of loving and cherishing to the idea of trading and obscenity of some kind, illustrates our ambivalence when it comes to trusting those we love and the unease we experience at our own sexuality.

Desdemona's tragedy

In Shakespeare's *Othello*, we witness that slide in action. It is the story of a mixed marriage, between a man of colour – a general who has pledged his service and his valour to Venice – and a beautiful white Venetian woman. When we first meet Othello, he is the embodiment of the romantic hero; as Professor Wilson Knight writes in his famous study of Shakespearean tragedy, *The Wheel of Fire*:

> Othello radiates a world of romantic, heroic and picturesque adventure. All about him is highly coloured. He is a Moor; he is noble and generally respected; he is proud in the riches of his achievements; his prowess as a soldier is emphasized ... Desdemona is his divinity – she is expressly feminine – we hear of her needlework, her fan, her gloves ...

At the beginning of the play Othello seems to worship Desdemona and believe in her virtue above all things – she is everything to him. But the marriage that appears to have been made in heaven goes hellishly wrong when the evil Iago decides to poison his General's mind by planting seeds of doubt about Desdemona's sexual fidelity. Iago's personal beliefs, revealed to us in his soliloquies, are that humankind is worth nothing, that we are all obsessed with sex and that we have no ideals that cannot be shattered by our base appetites. He notices the high esteem in which another soldier, Cassio, holds Desdemona. Throughout the play, Cassio is always respectful and never over-familiar with her. Iago, in his own diseased imagination, believes that Cassio wishes to have sex with Desdemona, and that she in her turn will respond, as Cassio is a young, handsome man. Gradually, he convinces Othello that Desdemona and Cassio are having an affair.

Looking for proof

A key player in the great tragedy is a handkerchief embroidered with strawberries – a precious heirloom that belonged to Othello's mother, and which he has given to Desdemona. She understands the precious significance of the token and always keeps it with her. Iago persuades Emilia, his wife and Desdemona's maid, to steal the handkerchief, which he plants in Cassio's room. A scene then plays out involving Bianca, described in the cast list as a 'Courtesan, in love with Cassio'; Iago describes her in less flattering terms:

> A huswife that by selling her desires
> Buys herself bread and clothes; it is a creature
> That dotes on Cassio, as 'tis the strumpet's plague
> To beguile many and be beguiled by one …

'Strumpet', 'courtesan' and, strangely enough, the word 'huswife' are all different names for a whore. With these degrading terms, Iago indirectly debases Desdemona.

It is the courtesan who finds Desdemona's prized handkerchief in Cassio's chamber. This couldn't be better from Iago's point of view; he has Othello watch as Bianca accuses Cassio of seeing another woman, brandishing the embroidered handkerchief at him as proof of his infidelity. The linking of Bianca and Desdemona – in Othello's mind they are now equal, both 'whores' – is the nail in the coffin of his love for his unsuspecting wife.

In the fateful last act of the play Othello smothers Desdemona, after speaking to her in tones of the most alarming and ghastly contempt:

> Was this fair paper, this most goodly book,/ Made to write
> 'whore' upon? What committed!/ O thou public commoner!
> I should make very forges of my cheeks,/ That would to
> cinders burn up modesty,/ Did I but speak thy deeds …
> Impudent strumpet!

When the poor victim of his abuse cannot believe he is speaking to her with such brutality, he turns to her with absolute hatred:

I cry you mercy then;/ I took you for that cunning whore of Venice/ That married with Othello./ You, mistress, that should have the office opposite to Saint Peter,/ And keep the gate of hell!

The Othello Syndrome

Psychologists refer to pathological jealousy as the 'Othello Syndrome', and it is easy to see why. Regarding another human being as a possession has been a long-held tradition in certain cultures, and it is no coincidence that stories from these cultures can show horrifying illustrations of brutality, degradation and suffering in the name of 'honour'. In his study *Jealousy*, Peter Van Sommers writes about the 'societies of honour and shame', and points out the difference between the concept of male honour and female honour:

> Male honour tends to be active and competitive – should it be compromised, it can be reconstructed. Female honour and shame are, by contrast, passive and defensive, and once lost, cannot be reclaimed. Women are widely regarded as not just weak and vulnerable, but as active sources of potential dishonour. It is not necessary for women to take any particular action to have this effect. According to [J.K.] Campbell, the attitude in Northern Greece was that 'even unconsciously, she may lure a man to disaster without a glance or gesture'.

In his book *Honour and the Devil*, J.K. Campbell describes the women of this region dressed completely in black, and compelled by protocol to move slowly and never to run. To fall might risk public dishonour. Van Sommers quotes Campbell further: 'A girl who is seen running risks ridicule and a reputation for shamelessness. If, by some evil chance, she were to fall backwards with her legs in the air, she would virtually lose her honour.'

The Bada Bing

The Mafia, such a society of honour and shame, is the subject of one of the most popular series ever to be shown on television, *The Sopranos*. Episode 32 contains one of the most shocking scenes in television history. Tracee, one of the naked 'pole' dancers at Tony Soprano's 'Bada Bing' strip club, has become involved with Ralph Cifaretto, one of the 'made men' of the Mafia. Ralph could aptly be described as a psychopath. Without the slightest shred of empathy, compassion or remorse, he meets all the diagnostic criteria for anti-social personality disorder. He cannot even comply with the rules of the Mob; he is deceitful, impulsive, irritable and aggressive, and exhibits 'reckless disregard for the safety of himself or others' (*Diagnostic and Statistical Manual of the American Psychiatric Association*). He shows no honour – not even honour among thieves – and is completely indifferent to the appalling mistreatment he doles out to other human beings. The power held by Tony Soprano is almost unbearable for him. (A great tribute to the acting talent of Joe Pantoliano – the manic tension Ralph exhibits when Tony pulls rank is nigh on tangible!)

In Episode 32 of *The Sopranos* we get to know the childlike Tracee, a 20-year-old single mother with the body of a well-endowed supermodel. We see her approach Tony and offer him a home-baked date loaf as thanks for some advice he has given her about her son. Tracee senses Tony's potential as a kindly father and, desperate for any crumb of love or nurture, she follows him around longingly. When Tracee goes missing from the Bada Bing, we discover she is living with Ralphie and is pregnant with his baby. One of Tony's cohorts turns up and literally drags poor Tracee by the hair back to the Bada Bing for 'duty'. Ralphie watches her being abused and laughs.

Later there is a gathering at the Bada Bing, and a scene emerges during which Tracee makes indignant and slightly offensive remarks to Ralph in front of the other guys. She leaves the club and we see her standing in the carpark, smoking a cigarette. Ralph follows, hate flaming in his eyes. For a few minutes he plays out a charade of the caring lover, assuring her he wants to take care of her and the baby. Suddenly, his face twists into the terrifying mask of the true psychopath, and he tells Tracee that if the baby is a girl, she will 'grow up to be a cock-sucking slob like her mother'. Ineffectually, Tracee takes a couple of swipes at Ralph. There ensues one of the most gruesome and brutal scenes ever played out on a television screen. In what bears a strong resemblance, because of the quasi-documentary style of *The Sopranos*, to a real-life 'snuff' video, we witness an immature, naive and fragile girl being beaten unrelentingly to death. We hear her bones cracking, her organs disintegrating, as Ralphie kicks and pounds her.

'Some dead whore'

'He's killed her,' I remember my husband saying as we watched. He said it as if we were watching a real incident. For several days afterwards I felt some post-trauma symptoms – I couldn't stop replaying the scene in my mind and had nightmarish dreams around the episode. We also see how shocked and distressed Tony Soprano feels – the anti-hero, our touchstone, the man with whom we somehow identify, who is at the same time a husband, father, patient, captain of the Mob, murderer and lover. He is deeply traumatised by the horrible murder of the poor girl. However, in order to keep the code of 'honour' of the Mafia, he can only object to the fact that Ralphie has 'disrespected the Bing' – in other words that he committed the act of murdering Tracee on the 'hallowed ground' of Tony's club, the main 'sit-down' venue for the Mob. We see how disgusted Tony feels, and he hits Ralph, a total violation of Mob rules – one 'made guy' doesn't hit another. 'Rules are rules,' Ralph says in righteous indignation: 'All this over some dead whore'.

The rules of the Mafia are not about honouring another person's life, but about internal protocol. Tracee's life is worth nothing, because she is a 'whore'. Tony feels differently, seeing her as a poor kid who reminds him poignantly of his own daughter. Later in the episode he astonishes his daughter by taking her by the shoulders, making direct eye contact with her, and telling her he loves her more than anything in the world – totally uncharacteristic behaviour. Yet his power to object to the murder of the 'poor kid' Tracee is limited by the lack of value her life holds in the culture that governs him. In this culture women are worthy of respect only if they are meticulously faithful to the men they have married.

The femme fatale

The idea of women tempting men into dishonour goes right back to the story of Adam and Eve. If we see the apple as representing sensual pleasure, then from the very beginning of storytelling, women are seen as luring men into evil and ruin. Van Sommers describes the Algerian Arabs referring to their women as 'the cows of Satan'. The idea of the danger of women, especially beautiful, sensual women, has been explored in countless songs, novels, plays, operas and poems. The 'femme fatale' took on a new lease of life from 1990 in a number of Hollywood movies where sexually provocative women suddenly metamorphose into crazed killers. *Basic Instinct* is such a film. In the role that made her a star, Sharon Stone plays a highly charged, predatory woman, who literally wrecks men's lives with her insatiable sexual appetite. The suggestion is that she lures them to certain death.

Like the Sirens in Greek mythology, beautiful, sensual women are often portrayed as agents of destruction. The Sirens sing and play the sweetest music. Winged beauties, they lace their songs with hidden meanings, causing passing sailors to feel compelled to stay and listen. The island on which they live is full of the bones of shipwrecked mariners. In the Coen brothers' brilliant allegoric homage to Homer, the 2000 film *Oh Brother, Where Art Thou?* the Sirens are lovely, languorous girls, combing their long hair, and singing the hypnotic lullaby 'Go to Sleep You Little Baby'. The sensual, alluring woman is also the mother of babies.

Christiane Olivier sees a direct link between the man's fear of women's overt sexuality (which leads, perhaps, to infidelity) and that first relationship with mother. She writes in Jocasta's Children:

> He has not forgotten the intense exchanges with that first woman. Was it not to her that he used to say, long ago and in all innocence, 'I'm going to marry you when I grow up?' And did he not have to back down in favour of a rival, his father? For she was married to this father, even if she sometimes seemed to prefer the son. But the father was the rival who could not be dislodged, and the man goes on living in fear that his woman will be taken away from him by another man.

The mother's betrayal

Paul is a forensic pathologist. He decided on a career to do with 'crime' after reading Truman Capote's book about a real-life home invasion and brutal killing of an entire family, *In Cold Blood*, at the age of 13:

> That book blew me away – I mean it blew me away! It wasn't just anger at the slaughter of the family – which was unbelievably barbaric. It was Capote's sense of injustice at how the perpetrators were treated – he went into great detail about their lives up to the crime – they were extremely

deprived – there was something inevitable about it – it made
a massive impression on me …

Paul's confusion about whether to see things from the point of view of victim or perpetrator makes sense when the intensely painful events of his childhood are taken into account. His father went off with another woman when Paul was four, leaving his mother to bring up the three children alone. Resources were scarce, and Paul knew all about deprivation:

As far as my mother was concerned, I felt starved of her love
when I was small, and that was because I *was* starved of it.
Mom always took more of an interest in my sister than in
either me or my brother, but I don't think that any of us felt
particularly wanted. She used to tell us regularly that she
hoped to win the pools so that she could afford to have us all
put in children's homes, and I remember dreading that this
would one day happen.

When Paul was nine, his mother met a swimming instructor down at the local baths. This young man of 17 became his mother's lover, and eventually her second husband. Paul remembers many occasions when he would return from school to find all the doors locked, knowing this meant he would have to stay out in the garden until his mother and her young boyfriend had finished their lovemaking and would reluctantly allow the children to come inside. This would happen rain or shine. Once the couple were married, the boy stepfather would abuse the boy children in a number of ways. Paul remembers being dragged out of bed in the middle of the night and accused of not cleaning up properly. He would then be beaten and made to polish cutlery until the early hours of the morning. It is hard for him to connect with the extreme pain he was in at that time of his life. His tendency is to intellectualise and stand back. He weighs up the evidence, as he is used to doing in his work:

> Mom's marriage to her second husband was extremely divisive. It quickly became apparent that he would never feel for the children of her first marriage like a father should. Worse than that though, we were perceived to be in the way – a drain on the family's limited financial resources – and my stepfather had taken on three of someone else's children at a very young age. Mom did seem to deeply love him – in sharp contrast with my Dad – who I don't think she ever loved or liked that much at all. In such a divisive environment, she often had to choose between her husband and her children, and I don't feel that she chose us.

Every boy is confronted by the cold fact that Mum is going to choose Dad over him. In Paul's case, the confrontation was horribly brutal. In her exploration of male fantasies, *Men in Love*, Nancy Friday describes the everyday variety of the confusion and frustration boys experience at puberty: 'Mother used to tenderly tuck you into bed at night, reproving you gently for trying to put your hand on her nightgowned breast. Then she blandly went off to share a bed with dad.'

For Paul, there was never any tenderness. For him, there was no reconciling himself that Mother was going off with the other loved parent. Instead, he experienced the acute pain of rejection and disparagement by his mother time and time again, and the unequivocal knowledge that he would always lose out to that other boy – the boy his mother took into her bed so eagerly:

> I remember during one therapy session that you observed that you were convinced that I wanted my stepfather dead. It didn't occur to me at the time you said it, but I remembered subsequently an occasion when I felt that wish, and I voiced it

to another. I remember where I was and to whom I was talking, very clearly indeed. I was 16, and my mother had just endured my stepfather leaving her for another woman, and had agreed to kick me out because this was a prerequisite for him to return.

The presenting past

Paul's presenting issue when he consulted me was that he felt unable to make satisfactory relationships with women because of extreme jealousy. He would experience nightmares, fantasies and obsessional thoughts involving the infidelity of his current partner, images that showed themselves to him in minute detail – he would see lips meet in slow motion, clothes removed, passionate lovemaking between his partner and some other man – and experience emotionally the very real pain he had felt as a child and a teenager. He would fly into a jealous rage – like Othello – and call his partner a whore. Despite his extraordinary levels of control in other areas of his life, over this particular area he felt powerless and as if he was going to lose his mind.

We learn from our experience. Paul's experience was that the woman to whom he was supposed to mean so much treated him as if he had no value. He learned that his father wasn't valued either. He learned that his mother was prepared to abandon him at a moment's notice. He learned that he would never be preferred to his rival – that other boy who had managed to usurp his mother's bed. How can he trust a woman's love? He still has no answer to this question. His refuge from suffering has continued to be his intellectual ability, his work:

The sanctuary in which I took refuge as a child was
educational achievement – I excelled at school. This carried a

universal respect, and to some extent, compensated for loneliness and feelings of inadequacy in virtually all the other areas of my life.

Richard O'Neill Dean says in 'Falling in (to the need for) Love':

Always we are trying to let go or recover from the deep and frightful injuries of our infancy and early childhood. To climb out of falling in love, one must see clearly that it is based on a need for love, and attendant illusory belief that this need will be met.

Paul's story illustrates how the deep injuries he experienced turned into an overwhelming need to have a loving woman who belongs to him, and to him alone. Yet the painful gift of his active and highly tuned imagination can't allow him ever to believe that need could be fulfilled, for his experience has proved that it will be just the reverse. Didn't he long to be valued and cherished by his mother long ago? And didn't she betray him in the most overt and brutal way? Paul is convinced in the core of his being that all women are whores. The betrayal of his mother and subsequent women with whom he has been involved has hardened his heart, and led him to exist in a state of isolated cynicism: 'Trust in the general populace declines with experience. I don't have much love for the human race these days.'

Early betrayal by mother can have devastating effects on male/female relationships, particularly when it is linked to exposure to overt sexuality. Freud describes the difficulty experienced by any child whose mother becomes pregnant and gives birth to another baby:

A child who has been put into second place by the birth of a brother or sister, and who is now, for the first time, almost isolated from his mother, does not easily forgive her this loss of place; feelings which in an adult would be described as

greatly embittered arise in him and are often the basis of
permanent estrangement.

The bitter feelings Freud speaks of are also to do with the indisputable
proof that mother has been intimately involved, sexually involved,
with 'the other man'. In Paul's case, the other man was not a father with
whom he also had a loving and intense involvement, but a boy only a
few years older than him. Linked with the 'estrangement' is an
awareness of mother's sexuality. This is an uncomfortable area for most
children, but when it is as confronting, rejecting and brutal as it was
for Paul, the mistrust of women and their sexuality can be lasting and
severe.

Tony's panic attacks

Tony Soprano suffers from panic attacks, the first of which happened
as his father was romancing his mother round the dinner table.
American psychoanalyst Glen Gabbard writes about the episode in the
following terms in his brilliant exposé of the series, *The Psychology of
the Sopranos*:

> He sees his dad hugging his mother from behind as they sit
> down at the dinner table with one of Mr Satriale's succulent
> roasts. As Johnny Boy hugs Livia, he sings 'All of me – why
> not take all of me?' in his most seductive voice. As he dances
> with her, he intones 'the lady loves her meat'. Johnny Boy cuts
> the roast, and Tony has his first fainting episode.

Later in the series, we see Tony's son have a fainting episode too, again
at around 13 years of age. Anthony Junior is standing resplendent in
his uniform for the military college to which Tony has decided to exile
him. Tony and his wife Carmela are both commenting on AJ's

appearance. Carmela is admiring her son, and says with a longing look: 'If I weren't already married …' AJ passes out.

The heady perfume of mother's sexual availability is too strong and too confusing, even when her partner is the boy's own dad. If there is any suggestion – and there often is – that she might also be available to her son, this can result in longstanding difficulties with intimacy. In *Jocasta's Children,* Christiane Olivier speaks of 'the frantic chase after male desire' which dominates the life of many women, and can result in a strange flirtatiousness towards her own son, or a flaunting of her sexuality:

> The woman will sexualise whatever can be seen by the other.
> Since her sex got no recognition when she was a little girl, the
> woman will take on her whole body as a sexual signal, and
> then will be afraid to display it. It will be said of her that she
> becomes hysterical because she appeals continually to the
> gaze of the other to guarantee her sexual identity. What a
> difference there is between her and the man – the man is
> given this desiring gaze from the outset, by his mother.

So we begin to understand the great ambivalence with which men regard the overtly sexual woman.

The beast with two backs

Looking back to that other saga of Italian domestic tension, we can observe that from the very beginning of the play Othello's relationship with Desdemona is portrayed in explicitly sexual terms. As her father learns about the growing love between his white daughter and the black general, he is told: '… an old black ram is tupping your white ewe'.

Later the lovemaking is described again in shockingly primitive language: '... your daughter and the Moor are now making the beast with two backs'. As Jan Kott writes in his essay 'The Two Paradoxes of Othello', in *Shakespeare Our Contemporary*:

> The image of the animal with two backs, one white, the other black, is one of the most brutal, and at the same time, one of the most fascinating representations of the sexual act. Othello is fascinated by Desdemona, but Desdemona is much more fascinated by Othello. She gives up everything, she is in a hurry, she does not want a single empty night any more.

Kott argues that it is not just Iago's malevolent persuasion that arouses Othello's unquenchable fire of jealousy and hatred, but also his growing unease around Desdemona's enthusiastic passion:

> The more intensely Desdemona becomes engrossed by love, the more of a slut she seems to Othello – a past, present and future slut. The more she desires, the better she loves, the more readily Othello believes that she can, or has, betrayed him. Desdemona is the victim of her own passion. Her love testifies against her, not for her. Love proves her undoing.

Othello seems to epitomise the man caught in a dark trap of love, desire, jealousy and disgust – what is to stop the desirable woman, the desiring woman, desiring someone else, just as, long ago, mother did? If a woman is desirable, the man is instantly at risk, especially if his self-esteem is fragile; if he, like Othello, feels like an outcast in the society or the culture in which he lives. The old sixties song by Dr Hook says it succinctly:

> When you're in love with a beautiful woman, you watch her eyes.
> When you're in love with a beautiful woman, you look for lies ...

Maybe it's just an ego problem
Problem is I've been fooled before ...

Never before have these difficulties between men and women been as exaggerated as they are today. The emphasis on appearance poses many problems in our relationships with each other. Rosemary McLeod, the New Zealand cartoonist, summed it up in her 'Strange Phenomena of Our Times' series. The little picture shows a curvy and voluptuous young blonde woman in the tiniest bikini. The young woman is blushing and frowning, looking cross. The caption is: 'The girl who hates men staring at her'. This seems to encapsulate the tension between men and women perfectly. The term 'provocatively dressed' is usually applied to women, and the whole idea of provocation assumes that a set of undesirable feelings are being evoked which, once let loose, cannot be controlled. The beautiful woman can be seen as the temptress, the goddess, the bitch, and the whore, while remaining curiously distant from any connection with sexual feelings.

Marilyn

Immensely appealing, immensely disturbing, Marilyn Monroe's shiny-lipped giggle as her white skirts blow up around her beautiful breasts remains one of the most haunting images of the last century. Similarly, the long-dead Princess Diana, looking up through her eyelashes as the magazine headline screams 'Diana's Secret Sex Life', still pulls the crowds and sells the tabloids. As women, we are drawn and compelled by the conundrum of how to attract, while men are not sure whether to be aroused or afraid.

Gloria Steinem, one of many writers to look at the desperately sad life of Marilyn Monroe, writes movingly of the chasm between the sex-goddess image Marilyn portrayed and the needs and longings that belonged to her alter ego, Norma Jeane:

By her own testimony, Marilyn didn't find sexual satisfaction with either men or women. Her sexual value to men was the only value she could be sure of. By exciting and arousing, she could turn herself from the invisible, unworthy Norma Jeane into the visible, worthwhile Marilyn. She could have some impact, some power, some proof that she was alive. Marilyn kept hoping that a relationship with a man would give her the identity she lacked, and that her appearance would give her the man. This impossible search was exaggerated by a society that encourages women to get their identity from men, and encourages men to value women for their appearance, not mind or heart.

The facts of Marilyn's childhood are well-known – born out of wedlock in the 1920s to a young, vulnerable and emotionally unstable mother, she was raised by a series of neighbours and aunts, spending time in foster homes and orphanages. Marilyn grew up unable to know or even contact her father, and in her mind he became an amalgam of all the great movie stars of the time. Men had all the power in Hollywood, and Marilyn longed to be a beloved daughter. Gloria Steinem quotes from Marilyn's autobiography about her feelings when she was shown a photograph of her father:

'I was so excited I almost fell off the chair. It felt so good to have a father, to be able to look at his picture and know I belonged to him. That was my first happy time …' From then on, she conjured up fantasies that she would replay over and over. When Norma Jeane walked home from school in the rain, she imagined her father waiting and worrying that she might have got wet. Lying in hospital with complications after having her tonsils removed, his abandoned daughter imagined this handsome man entering the ward 'while the other patients looked on in disbelief and envy … and I gave him dialogue too – you'll be well in a few days, Norma Jeane,

I'm very proud of the way you're behaving, not crying all the time like the other girls.'

Marilyn's yearning to have a father's love and tenderness led her to dress, walk, talk and sing in ways she knew would appeal to men:

'As soon as I could afford an evening gown,' she remembered, 'I bought the loudest one I could find. It was a bright red, low-cut dress, and my arrival in it infuriated half the women present. I was sorry, in a way, to do this, but I had a long way to go, and I needed a lot of advertising to get there.' In return for help from agents and studio executives, she gave in sexually again. Referring to the variety of love-making that men who are old or powerful or fond of degrading women seem to prefer, she later confessed, 'I spent a great deal of time on my knees.'

Towards the end of her life, Marilyn agreed to tell her story to the British journalist W.J. Weatherby. Here are her own words about the struggle experienced by many women – the overwhelming wish to be adorable, desirable and appealing, coupled with the yearning to be respected – recorded in *Conversations with Marilyn*:

Sometimes I've got such lousy taste in men. There was a whole period when I felt flattered if a man took interest in me – any man! I believed too easily in people, and I went on believing in them even after they disappointed me over and over again. I must have been very stupid in those days. I guess I'm capable of doing it again with some guy, though he'd have to be someone more outstanding than a heel. Not that I didn't pay for it all – all I've ever done. There were times when I'd be with one of my husbands, and I'd run into one of those Hollywood heels at a party, and they'd paw me cheaply in front of everybody, like they were saying, Oh we had her! I guess it's the classic situation of an ex-whore, though I never was a whore in that sense of the word, I was never kept – I always kept myself. But there was a period when I responded too much to flattery, and slept around too much, thinking it would help my career. The guys were always so full of self-confidence, and I had none at all and they made me feel better. But you don't get self-confidence that way. You have to earn it, by earning respect.

The shifting of our longings continues to make its kaleidoscopic patterns of light and shade. How can we trust the object of desire? We have all been hurt too much in the beginning by the explicit and implicit messages from the beloved parent. Mother rejects son, father rejects daughter. Confusing and ambivalent messages form the patchwork quilt that lies on the bed of our adult relationships.

Tammy's story
Billy Collins, in his wonderful poem 'Victoria's Secret', describes a man thumbing through the famous underwear catalogue, responding to each of the provocative models in their sexy lingerie:

> Stretched out catlike on a couch
> In the warm glow of a panelled library
> Is one who wears a distinctly challenging expression,
> Her face tipped up, exposing
> Her long neck, her perfectly flared nostrils,
> Go ahead, her expression tells me,
> Take off my satin charmeuse gown
> With a sheer jacquard bodice
> Decorated with a touch of shimmering Lurex.
> Go ahead, fling it into the fireplace,
> What do I care, her eyes say, we're all going to hell anyway.

The verse captures with such grace and wit the conundrum of the sexual tension between men and women. Do provocative dress and alluring expressions signify an invitation to have sex? The relationship between the prostitute and her client takes the doubt away. It is quite clear that a deal is being put on the table. The deal is explicit, as well as implicit – no more does the man have to wonder, to fear rejection. He just has to pay. Tammy worked as a prostitute for twenty years. Her sexual invitations were unequivocal:

> At work, I dressed to get clients – that's why they call you a hooker – you have to hook. I had a little black mini skirt, stockings, suspender belt, fishnets and big, big shoes. I wore tight tops to show off my breasts – I knew I had to dress to hook men – very sexually, you know? And my hair has always been long and blonde.

The deal was also unequivocal, and quite clearly set out from the very beginning of the meeting. Having established that a man was booking her, Tammy would clarify the terms:

> I'm an honest person. I'd say – OK – let's just relax and have a lovely time, but we don't do this and we don't do that – you have an established set of rules. And as prostitution changed, it became easier to work. There's a set price list now – you know sex is so much, and hand relief is so much and oral etc.

Tammy was completely honourable about the service aspect of the job – she was providing a service to her clients and wanted that service to be as good as she could make it:

> I learned how to massage, and got really good at that, so I could help them to relax and lie still. Then I'd do the teasing part, the talking to excite them. I was fun for them – I played

> their games. They loved the sex I gave them – it was so
> planned and professional, so polished. You become very
> skilled at it. If you worked as an artist for 20 years, you'd get
> very good at drawing pictures. I worked as a hooker for 20
> years, and I was very skilled at doing it. I was very beautiful,
> too, when I was younger.

Men got what they paid for. Tammy could be trusted to deliver an excellent service. The problems came when clients wanted more than they had paid for:

> Your regulars are having a love affair with you. For one guy, he
> thought I was his girlfriend. He would bring me flowers and
> call me honey, and treat me like a girlfriend, but then he had
> some really kinky things with sex, so he would change from
> being my boyfriend to being very demanding and a little bit
> bizarre.

Tammy knew that while her clients might be able to trust her, she could never trust them. With her background of having been sexually abused as a child, raped at 14 by a group of boys she knew as friends, and told repeatedly by her mother that she was 'only good for sex', Tammy knew that she had to look out for her own safety at all times:

> You've always got to be on the alert – you can never really
> relax, so the whole time you are faking this whole sex thing
> with your eyes shut, you're so on the alert, because any minute
> you could be under attack. I've been raped and beaten at
> work – I don't think I've ever trusted a male in my whole life.

Tammy avoided getting involved with regular clients. She preferred to work with men who wanted her sexually rather than emotionally:

You get regulars, but I tried not to have that many, because they want to attach, and I didn't like to attach. I had one for years who was besotted with me sexually, and I could talk him into whole day things – we'd have caviar and champagne – he'd buy me gifts and blankets and things when it was cold. But it wasn't love – it was different – it was only ever sexual with him.

Like Marilyn Monroe, Tammy never enjoyed the sex. The way she survived in the job was to develop another personality, a part of herself she called Josie:

She's fabulous – glamorous and confident. If I were to be raped, she'd have the sex for me, so Tammy wouldn't have to be sexually or physically abused. Josie would take it for her. Quick on her feet, quick with her tongue. Over the years, it became very divided – Tammy with no make-up and sober and scared, anxiety attacks and no confidence – Josie who didn't give a shit about anything, didn't have serious relationships, could cope with everything – just wrap men around her little finger, and was the soul of the party – she was much more fun.

The contract

Clients who deluded themselves that sex with a prostitute was not about buying a service might have felt bitterly disappointed to know the truth:

They develop a relationship with a fake entity, a non-person. It's not really who you are at all, so they are developing a relationship with a facade. One girl would bake six chocolate cakes and ice them all and bring them to work, and say – 'Look, I baked this just for you, because I was thinking about you all week.' Every client that day – 'Look – I baked this just for you!' She'd do different things like that all the time with her clients – she was so busy and so popular and they were all so in love with her. She was a junkie. Junkies work harder for their money because they need their money more to pay for their addictions.

The Nobel Prize-winner J.M. Coetzee's main character in his great novel *Disgrace* sees a prostitute called Soraya every Thursday night:

Soraya is tall and slim, with long black hair and dark, liquid eyes. Technically he is old enough to be her father … he has been on her books for over a year; he finds her entirely satisfactory. In the desert of the week, Thursday has become an oasis of luxe et volupte.

Soraya seems to be the answer to David's prayers. As a young man he could guarantee attracting the woman of his choice with his looks and charisma, yet as he's aged he's found it necessary to pursue women, or 'in one way or another, to buy them'. He feels fulfilled by his ninety minutes a week with the beautiful, compliant Soraya; it's all very relaxing and blissful:

Because he takes pleasure in her, because his pleasure is unfailing, an affection has grown up in him for her. To some degree, he believes, this affection is reciprocated. Affection may not be love, but it is at least its cousin. Given their unpromising beginnings, they have been lucky, the two of them: he to have found her, she to have found him.

David persists in this happy fantasy of reciprocal love until one day he sees Soraya out shopping with two boys who look just like her. He thinks they are her sons. He sees her in her own life, and is fascinated. He watches her go into a restaurant and walks past the window to look at her with her children. He walks back again a second time, and this time, Soraya sees him. Their eyes meet. After that, things cool between them. The trust has been damaged somehow – both are aware of the 'double life' they are each leading. One day, Soraya tells David she is taking a break and doesn't know when she'll be back. After some days, he phones the agency – they tell him Soraya has left. He tries other prostitutes from the agency's books, but he longs for Soraya. Eventually he decides to pay a detective to find her:

> Within days, he has her real name, her address, her telephone number. He telephones at nine in the morning, when husband and children will be out.
> 'Soraya,' he says. 'This is David. How are you? When can I see you again?'
> A long silence before she speaks. 'I don't know who you are,' she says. 'You are harassing me in my own house. I demand you will never phone me again here, never!'
> Demand – she means command. Her shrillness surprises him: there has been no intimation of it before. But then, what should a predator expect when he intrudes into the vixen's nest – into the home of her cubs?

David has made the mistake of confusing Soraya's professional self, who offers him a service for which he pays, with the person of Soraya who lives her own, completely separate, life with her family. To trust a whore's oath is to know what to trust. To trust that a whore will offer the service for which she is paid is one thing; to expect that she means it when she calls you the only one, and tells you she loves you, is another.

Legitimate rights

For many years, Tammy found it impossible to make a relationship with anyone. Because of the extreme suffering she had experienced in her own life, she expected to be despised:

> I was very abused at home. Mum was quite violent and locked me in a room a lot and told me she hated me and used to beat me quite often. I just hid in a wardrobe. I had anxiety attacks at three years old. I didn't get the support and comfort I should have had, you know?

Later she was abused further when, as a teenager, she went to work at a massage parlour:

> I was treated like a slave – had to do all the cleaning and work for hours and hours. They treated us so badly – we weren't allowed breaks. I left one shift and went straight to hospital. They'd made me do eight clients and I was sick – I just collapsed in the end.

Today Tammy works as a personal trainer and has learnt to feel good about herself. Her bond with the other girls throughout the years, which often kept her going, has led her to a fulfilling relationship with her partner Annie:

> She loves me as a person. She treats me with total respect – she told me I was really intelligent and she really likes who I am. She's just a lovely, very honest, very trusting person with a heart of absolute gold. Financially for a whole year she supported me and it cost her a lot of money. It was Annie and Josie that got together – I had so just become Josie when I met her – I didn't want to be Tammy any more because it was

just too painful. But Annie saw Tammy and she really loved her. Right from the beginning she liked Tammy and no-one else ever has really.

Although life at times can be hard, and Tammy sometimes feels a pull to go back to her former life, she knows she will not go back to working as a prostitute. She has to take care not to get overwhelmed by other people's opinions:

If I spend too much time with my family, I can go downhill quite rapidly – I have to be careful of that, because they still call me a drunken whore. If I listen to that, my mind can still head off there. I just don't act on it. I can say different things to myself now.

In many countries, new laws have recently been passed protecting sex workers against abuse by operators of massage parlours and escort agencies. Under these laws, sex workers also have the right to refuse a potentially abusive client. Legislation has been put in place to decriminalise and protect prostitutes. Sex workers have the same legal status as their clients. The 'whore's oath' can be redefined as a clear contract between two people in recognition that one is buying and one providing a service.

Chapter 8

Self-trust and Self-doubt

Makeover

'Tell me what you don't like about yourself,' the plastic surgeons say to their prospective patients in the latest American TV series, *Nip/Tuck*. It's a question most of us could answer quite easily – there's always something we don't like about our appearance. Yet how many of us would submit to major surgery in the pursuit of perfection? We watch in horror as subjects are extremely made over – noses are ripped apart and broken with hammers, vulnerable bellies are sliced and diced, entire faces are peeled off and pegged up. Never before has so much opportunity been available to us to completely remodel and restructure our faces and bodies. Never have so many cases of BDD (Body Dysmorphic Disorder) been referred to doctors and psychiatrists. BDD can be defined as an excessive preoccupation with an imagined or minor defect of a localised facial feature or body part. It can result in a downward spiral in the person's functioning – a refusal to socialise, a decline in intimate relationships and a disengagement with everyday life. People who suffer from BDD imagine that everyone notices the perceived 'fault' – in the worst cases, sufferers see themselves as ugly, misshapen and offensive to others.

Jane in the mirror

The woman who sits opposite me is one of those tall, willowy, elegant women who would look good dressed in a flour sack. She is 50, and looks about 36. Her face is memorable, classically beautiful, with nigh on perfect features. Her cheekbones are high and her brown eyes are slightly almond shaped. She has olive-toned skin and looks Mediterranean. Her bobbed, shining brown hair would grace a shampoo ad. She loves native American Indian jewellery and wears a lot of silver and turquoise. She has great personal style. 'My mother hated me,' she says matter of factly.

Jane's mother, Beatie, was born into a poor family in Ireland in 1918. Her father, Jane's grandfather, was a strange, wild sort of man. Tall and wiry, he worked from time to time as a sewing machine engineer, mending and fixing the old machines that all the women in the area used to make clothes for their children, or to supplement the meagre household income by dressmaking for wealthier folks. Beatie's mother was a fiery redhead who erupted regularly into violent rages and would thrash her four children whenever the mood took her. Beatie was the clever one of the family, and as she got older she escaped beatings because she was pretty and smart. As a woman, she was delicately built, with large round blue eyes and a Cupid's bow mouth; she looked rather like the famous forties film star Bette Davis. Beatie was one of the first women in the 1930s to get into Trinity College, Dublin, where she studied French Literature. In the old photographs that Jane brought in to show me, Beatie stands against one of the ancient stone walls of Trinity, her straight skirt fitting beautifully over her slim hips, her white frilled blouse tailored to show off her small, pert breasts. Her hair rolls back in shining waves from her high forehead, framing her pretty face. She is a doll.

In 1937, while at university, Beatie met a Jewish medical student. He was a refugee whose family had managed to escape Poland before the Nazi invasion. His name was Dov, after his Russian grandfather. Beatie reluctantly married him in 1939; 'He had me persecuted,' she would tell Jane. 'Wherever I went, there he was. He sat in my favourite cafes for hours just waiting for me to come in, he followed me, he begged me to marry him.' Beatie spent the rest of her life believing she had done Dov the most enormous favour. Dov spent the rest of his life adoring Beatie, spoiling her, pampering her and running around after her. He bought her clothes, jewellery, red roses. ('Why does your father buy me these bloody roses?' Jane remembered her mother saying; 'Their heads always droop after two days!')

After the war (Dov was in the Royal Army Medical Corps) they moved to a town in the east of England where Dov worked as a consultant physician. Beatie never worked; Dov didn't want her to – he wanted her to stay at home where he could find her. His strategy didn't work, for Beatie joined every committee she could find. She stood for the town council and won a seat. She was the star of local society, regularly seen smiling out from the newspapers. Jane told me bitterly:

> She was a very showy large goldfish in a small mossy pond. My father never stopped asking me where she was – 'Where's your mother?' – all the time. I used to feel like saying 'What about me? I'm here – won't I do?' But I knew that, in the adoration stakes, I had no chance at all – he only had eyes for her.

Jane was born in 1952, a little dark baby girl; Beatie had been hoping for a son. Beatie knew she could only have one baby – she had suffered from toxaemia and high blood pressure throughout the pregnancy. She was horribly disappointed with her daughter. She had also resented having to give up smoking and drinking her habitual three pink gins each evening. With tears in her eyes, Jane said:

> Do you know what the midwife who delivered me told me? My mother's first words when I left her body were 'Give me a fag, for the love of God!' The midwife told me she sounded like an old bag lady on the streets of Dublin! She never even asked if her baby girl was OK!

126

Dov seemed to love his little, dark, Russian baby well enough. Both her parents were so busy, though, that Jane hardly saw them and was always looked after by a cleaning lady – never the same one for long, as Beatie would offend her 'women' with her autocratic ways, getting them to call her 'madam' and meet her perfectionist standards. Beatie never had any time for Jane, and Jane's first memory was of the little rhyme her mother would chant: 'Before you came we had such fun, and now our work is never done!'

Dov would buy golden boxes of chocolate truffles along with the bottles of Gordon's gin when he did the shopping every Saturday. Beatie would hoard them away in a special cupboard. Never eating any proper meals, she didn't put on weight in spite of all the chocolate and gin. Jane remembers stealing chocolates and getting into no end of trouble. Her mother would call her a greedy fat pig and tell her she would never get a boyfriend.

Dov and Beatie spent all their spare money on five-star hotels, where Beatie would receive the treatment on which she thrived, being fawned on by the hotel staff and brought special drinks, afternoon teas and packets of cigarettes on silver trays. As a little girl Jane would have to sit in the formal dining rooms with their white starched tablecloths and silver cutlery and behave impeccably. Not surprisingly, as Jane approached puberty, an eating disorder took hold. Jane felt like throwing up every time she sat down to a meal. Like her mother, the only food she really enjoyed was chocolate. While Jane's school years were successful enough and she did quite well, her memories are of intense self-consciousness. She felt like a geek – ugly, brown, misshapen, gawky.

The fragile self

Phil Mollon, in his great study of narcissism, *The Fragile Self*, speaks of the phenomenology of self-consciousness, and writes of three varieties of self-consciousness:

1. Self-awareness, the ability to introspect and be conscious of one's self.
2. Embarrassed self-consciousness, a painful and shameful awareness of the self as the object of the other's unempathic attention.
3. A compulsive and hypochondriacal preoccupation with the self: a compelling need to look in mirrors and to evoke mirroring responses from others.

Mollon goes on to describe the advent of the 'emergence of a self that observes the self' which seems to occur in the second half of the second year of life. It is during this time that the child begins to show concern over behaviour that violates adult standards. It is similar to Carl Rogers' idea of those 'conditions of worth' that begin to infiltrate the organismic self, and distance the child from its own experience. When the child who is delighting in the experience of the muddy puddle is told sharply 'What a mess you are!' the result is a sudden onset of stage two – embarrassed self-consciousness. The more repetitive such unempathic interventions are when the self is being observed, the more disturbed is the interaction between self and others.

Beatie not only had no empathy for Jane, she constantly criticised her appearance, made disparaging comparisons between Jane and herself, and triumphed over her gleefully in an intense rivalry for Dov's regard and love. Jane knew she would always be the loser in this competition. Beatie told Jane she was 'a big-boned girl', 'not everyone's cup of tea', and called her a 'yakipak' (a Yiddish word for a dark, Sephardic Jew). As Jane began to reach young womanhood, her mother was becoming old and losing her prettiness. Beatie's petite figure began to be replaced by a pot belly and sagging flesh. Jane felt more and more hated. It was a classic *Snow White* situation, except that Beatie was Jane's mother, not her stepmother. In the old fairytale, the stepmother has to consult the mirror daily to be reassured that she is the most beautiful woman in the land. When one day the mirror tells her she is no longer the most beautiful, and that she has been outdone by the lovely young girl who is growing up in her house, she fragments into a psychotic, tortured state. The film *Snow White – A Tale of Terror*, starring Sigourney Weaver, shows this in the most emotional terms. The mirror represents the gaze of the world. As Phil Mollon says:

> When there is an experience or fantasy of an unempathic other observing the self, the more total the identification with the observing other, the more intense the self-consciousness. The presence of the other may be felt to be overwhelming, pushing the subjective self to the margin. Self-consciousness then emerges as a response to a threat to the self.

Jane's self was repeatedly threatened by the extreme and unpleasant self-involvement of her mother, and she suffered intensely from the envious attacks her mother would make on her. As a result, Jane became obsessed with her appearance. She continued to be successful in terms of her career – she went to university and became a lecturer at an art college – but, never confident enough to develop intimate relationships with friends or partners, Jane became increasingly unwell. The agonising self-doubt fostered by her mother's envy and dislike led her towards exploring options for changing the minutiae of her appearance that offended her, and that she imagined offended others.

Her first move was to book regular appointments at a beauty salon, where every hair on her body was painstakingly removed with hot wax. It seemed quite normal to have facial and pubic hair ripped out – lots of people do it regularly. Her beauty therapist helpfully suggested a process called dermabrasion to remove the tiny lines that Jane noticed forming on her upper lip. In this process, the practitioner scrapes away the outer layer of skin with a rough wire brush, or a burr made of diamond particles, attached to a motorised handle. After dermabrasion, the skin is red and swollen – eating and talking are very painful for the first few days. The skin eventually forms a scab-like crust, but the sensitivity and swelling can last for months. Although the whole thing was intensely painful, Jane felt very cared for and nurtured by the kindly older man who was her surgeon. He was dark like her, like Dov. He was probably Russian Jewish in origin. He was very concerned and attentive.

Obsession

Jane decided to go back to the same surgeon a few months later, when her skin had settled down, to have a lip implant. She had never liked her mouth – the top lip was too thin – and she looked longingly at the full, pouty lips of the Hollywood stars in the magazines. This time, her lip was sliced open from the inside, and a spongy piece of Teflon was inserted. For weeks afterwards Jane's mouth was numb and swollen, her face bruised and sore. She took extended leave without pay and stayed home, alone, until the swelling went down. Little by little, Jane was becoming an addict. Her first major operation involved liposuction from her stomach and thighs. She went on to have three separate rhinoplasty (nose job) operations, each time consulting a different surgeon; the results never satisfied her and she didn't want her first, favourite surgeon to think badly of her. This operation is done from inside the nose. Several cuts are made in the nostrils, and a chisel is used to reform the cartilage.

Despite the obvious pain and discomfort of such surgery, every time Jane walked into those luxurious offices she felt a sense of absolute calm and peace. The surgeons who attended her were charming and often very attractive. Her fantasies and dreams were of these doctors (who often reminded her of Dov, her father) and she became less and less inclined to seek the company of others. Her fantasies also involved the mirror which would one day reflect a confident, beautiful Jane who at last would have banished the image of the clumsy, dark-skinned changeling child her mother never wanted.

In the first episode of *Nip/Tuck*, a series based on the exploits of a plastic surgery practice in Florida, the unscrupulous Dr Christian Troy meets a beautiful, confident and sexy young model. At first she seems uninterested in him, but on learning his profession is eager to go with him to a hotel room. She tells him she is 21; he takes her over to the window and scrutinises her face in the daylight. 'Twenty-six,' he says; 'you should have used your sunscreen.' From there it is an easy trip into her inner doubts and fears. He tells her that far from being the 'perfect ten', she measures around eight out of ten on the perfection scale. He then proceeds to mark her lovely face with a felt-tip, showing her the little adjustments she needs to bring her face up to the level of perfection for which she longs. She is a lamb to the slaughter – for these little adjustments are not done with a felt-tip but a scalpel, cutting deeply into the flesh of her already exceptionally beautiful face. The mirror has become her enemy instead of her friend.

Narcissism explained

The myth of Narcissus is a familiar one to most of us. In his classic work *Metamorphosis*, the writer Ovid (43 BC–AD 17) tells us the story of a beautiful lad who was born to a river god and a nymph. The boy, whose physical beauty is beyond compare, has a magnetic appeal for both sexes. The nymph Echo falls obsessively in love with him and cannot resist following him and pleading with him to return her love. Eventually her body withers from lack of response and she becomes only a pleading voice. Narcissus continues to mock and scorn those who profess love for him. Eventually, he lies down by a pool and sees his own reflection. For the first time in his life Narcissus feels the torture of unrequited love, not realising that the object of his adoration is his own reflection. The reflection moves and shifts, seeming to torment him. He leans down to kiss the lovely face he sees rising up towards him, but as soon as his lips touch the water the reflection vanishes. Eventually, in agony, Narcissus too withers away and dies, still gazing at his own beloved reflection, just as Echo withered away from loving him:

> Then on the wholesome earth, he gasping lies,
> Till death shuts up those self-admiring eyes
> To the cold shades his flitting ghost retires,
> And in the Stygian waves, itself admires.

Dr Bruce Stevens, in his book *Mirror, Mirror*, a study of different types of narcissists, labels one 'The Body Shaper'. He talks about the very fragile sense of self that most people have when they become focused on their appearance in the way that Jane did. Jane achieved an almost perfect outward beauty and looked much younger than her 50 years, yet she was incapable of entering into an intimate relationship with another person. Just like the beautiful Narcissus, she spent long hours in the company of mirrors, gaining scant pleasure from the admiration and compliments she received from others. They were never enough: 'If the need for admiration is extreme, then the attention of only one person can soon lose value. There has to be an admiring crowd.'

Throughout the history of humankind, concern about appearance has been usual in the range of human anxieties, and specific standards of beauty have exerted their particular pressure across every culture. Studies have shown that attractive children are more popular, both with classmates and with teachers. Attractive applicants have a better chance of getting jobs and of receiving higher salaries. To be beautiful and good is to be desired, adored and cherished – the wish of every child. Princesses and fairies represent our wish to be adorable and wondrous creatures. Passionate love and beautiful appearances are often linked in movies, so we are led to believe that beautiful people make wonderful partners. In fact, the opposite is very often the case. As Dr Stevens says:

> The Body Shaper has a false assumption – everything is external – including the problem … grandiosity is always distorting in a relationship. This can happen if the Body Shaper begins to believe the positive feedback: 'If I receive so much admiration, I must be special' – admiration awakens need, as well as never satisfying it. The result is something like a growing tolerance for an addictive drug.

The result can be emotional withdrawal, continuing disappointment and a desperate need to conceal 'the truth' from a potential partner – the truth of aging, the truth of gaining a kilo here and there, the truth of the raging need inside for attention and nurturing that prevents the person from ever achieving psychological intimacy.

The power of beauty

Just as we tend to link beauty with virtue – the fairy princess is usually beautiful – so evil in myth and legend tends to have an ugly face. The wicked witch usually has a dreadful beaky nose, facial warts, and seems to be in the permanent grip of a bad hair day. Monsters can be seen as our fear of ugliness and deformity, our fear of being unloved and unlovable. Sometimes in fairytales the monster is transformed into a beautiful human being, as in *Beauty and the Beast*. In the Oscar-winning animated film *Shrek* the opposite happens. The eponymous hero is a green ogre, with dubious personal habits. Lord Farquaad is the short, self-obsessed villain of the piece, who consults a magic mirror to find out how to become a king. The mirror shows him a selection of beautiful trophy princesses so that he can gain credibility by marrying one of them. He chooses Princess Fiona, but neglects to listen to a vital piece of information the mirror tries to give him. Nightly, as the sun goes down, Princess Fiona turns into her true self – she becomes a green ogress. Shrek, sent to collect the princess and bring her back to Farquaad, falls in love with the beautiful Fiona with all his heart, although he knows his love can never be requited. One day her true appearance is revealed to him, but instead of being horrified, he is delighted – the relationship becomes real to him and he loves the ogress even more than he loved the doll-like princess. The delight of the many children who have responded so enthusiastically to this movie signals a ray of hope that perhaps in the next generation, the grip of our present rigid cultural definitions of beauty and value may loosen.

At this time, however, we are witnessing that grip becoming ever more unyielding. The magazines are brimming with stories of celebrity diets and plastic surgery as modern technology offers a vast selection of creams, injections, tattoos, implants and major operations in the quest for the perfectly desirable, ever-youthful human being. The Oscar ceremony has become a focus for millions of eyes to appraise and assess who is the fairest, the slimmest, the most toned and firm and supple of them all. When we look in the mirror, we don't just see our image staring back, we see the opinions of others – we experience the pain of being judged and shamed. The speaking mirror in *Snow White* warns us of the dangers of being over-involved with appearance. It tells us that this kind of obsessive quest to be the best and most beautiful is doomed to a tragic end. We must find our true worth through different means. Children need good mirroring to help them to form an identity – mirroring which helps them to feel worthwhile and proud of their individual gifts and abilities. When we have gained true confidence – belief and trust in ourselves as whole human beings – we can travel through the looking glass and find ourselves in the real world, where magic can happen in the exchange of reciprocal empathy and love with our fellow beings.

Sanity and madness

The themes of sanity and madness recur throughout the preceding chapters. To trust a wolf, to know about a horse's state of health, love and trust between men and women – all are feasible, and don't belong to the delusory world of the insane. It's an issue that has preoccupied humankind for so many years – the nature of sanity, the meaning of madness. Shakespeare, perhaps more than any other writer, examined and explored the concept of madness in his plays with an obsessive fascination.

In *King Lear*, the whole world seems full of madness. The Fool himself talks only in code, in riddles; Edgar, the son of a nobleman and the most eloquent and sensitive character in the play, voluntarily transforms himself into 'Poor Tom', a vagrant from the insane asylum of Bedlam, and from that point on joins the Fool in talking only in images. In the most powerful and haunting scene in the play, in the wild storm out on the moor, the blind and despairing Earl of Gloucester begs Poor Tom (who is really his son Edgar) to help him find the edge of a precipice so he may throw himself off it. Edgar leads him a little way on the flat moorland, then describes to him the drop from a huge cliff which is not there:

> Come on sir; here's the place: stand still./ How fearful and
> dizzy it is to cast one's eyes so low!/ The crows and choughs
> that wing the midway air/ Show scarce so gross as beetles …/
> The fishermen that walk upon the beach/ Appear like mice …

Gloucester believes it all – the description is so powerful. He imagines the height from which he must jump, his body falling hundreds of feet and joining those tiny beings one can scarcely see down on the beach. He throws himself off what he believes to be the cliff, and faints in the process. When he comes to, Edgar pretends to be someone at the bottom of the cliff who has just seen the amazing fall of the man who jumped. He pretends there has been a miracle that allowed Gloucester, despite his fall, to live, to survive against all odds:

Ten masts at each make not the altitude
Which thou hast perpendicularly fell.
Thy life's a miracle!

Crazier scenes can hardly be found in the history of theatre. And yet, in the middle of the craziness, we find an outstanding truth: what we believe can guide us through the worst nightmare, the greatest trauma. Gloucester begins to believe that his life has been miraculously saved because it is worth something. He no longer wants to die. He has self-worth. To trust ourselves – here is the greatest challenge of all. When I began working on this book I believed that self-worth was given or not given to us by our parents. It was to do with being valued, being trusted by others. Yet what I have discovered is that certain people, despite the worst circumstances and the most traumatic of events, manage to trust themselves and others with openness and certainty.

Michael Hurst's story

Michael Hurst is a New Zealand actor who is perhaps best-known for his portrayal of Iolaus in the American television series *Hercules* and its companion series *Xena, Warrior Princess*. When I spoke to Michael, he had just finished directing and starring in a superb production of Hamlet at Auckland's Maidment Theatre. The production was set in a timeless, nightmarish place, where young people in formal evening dress moved swiftly and nervously while the silver mask of the dead king stared down from the wall. The 'ghost scene', in which Hamlet sees the spirit of his dead father, was a truly terrifying experience, the stage cloaked in darkness, with beams of torchlight crossing and colliding. At one point one of the guards suddenly falls down, bleeding at the mouth and nose. He seems possessed, and the light changes to a pulsating and spectral heartbeat as the ghost speaks, telling his son the story of his 'murder most horrible'!

North by north-west

I was struck by the extraordinary courage of Michael's choices in the play, particularly those concerning the delivery of the unforgettable soliloquies (among them the most famous speech ever written, the one that begins 'To be or not to be …'). These speeches, often played as Hamlet's inner thoughts – as if he were speaking to himself, thinking out loud – were played directly to the audience with the lights full on. It seemed to me a striking example of self-trust, and I asked Michael how he reached that place of transparency and authenticity where he was able to make those well-worn lines sound as if they had never been said before. His answer was fascinating:

> I ook, I always knew that's how the soliloquies were going to be done for me. I should tell you that the way the production came to me, and the way that all my productions come to me, is that I get what I call 'a receive'. It downloads complete. It always downloads completely. Hamlet just went kaa-ching! The whole thing! The whole concept. Now, admittedly, I have done it before and I'm incredibly familiar with the lines and the whole play, but that's what happens. Now where that comes from, I don't know, but that's where the trust is for me.

Hamlet, like *King Lear*, is a play that deals with madness. Critics have argued for centuries about whether Hamlet becomes mad (driven to heartbreak by the murder of his father and the subsequent marriage of his mother to the perpetrator, his uncle) or whether he is 'feigning madness' in order to conceal his plans for revenge. In one of the play's many memorable lines, Hamlet says: 'I am but mad north-north-west: when the wind is southerly, I know a hawk from a handsaw.'

These words seem to illustrate perfectly the paradox of madness – how do we know a visionary from a neurotic, a delusion from a dream? Examples of crazy behaviour might be hearing voices or talking to someone who isn't there, yet we all experience these feelings or behaviours from time to time. Michael's Hamlet is a highly sensitive man who has been subjected to the most distressing experiences. He can trust no-one but himself:

> If it was in the real world, and you came into a room and you saw Hamlet doing a soliloquy, what you'd be seeing is a man talking to someone who wasn't there. Who is the audience to Hamlet? It's his imaginary friend.

Self-trust

Michael, like Hamlet, has been through times in his own life when there seemed to be no-one he could trust. To live in the imagination, in the world of his own beliefs, was his only option. Born in Lancashire in 1957, to 19-year-old parents, he was only 18 months old when his father left to fight the Mau Mau uprising in Kenya. Michael remembers kissing his dad's photo at night. But when his father returned there were perpetual fights between his parents, and by the time he was six Michael was in a gang and in trouble with the police for vandalism. The environment in which he was growing up was anything but empathic: 'I was never read to, never had a birthday party, never had any of that stuff, because they just didn't know about it, and they were too caught up in their own young, frustrated lives.'

Michael's creative spirit, however, stayed intact, and he knows that from a very early age that had a large amount to do with his innate talent for theatre:

I do remember being in a Catholic school in England. I must have been about four, because we started at four. We all had to be St George fighting the dragon, and I remember the nuns picking me to show everybody. I can tell you exactly why they picked me – it was because of my dragon. I just automatically saw this dragon – as big as a house – huge – and I thought, 'The only way I can kill this dragon is to get underneath and stick my sword into its soft underbelly.' I was ducking and diving and the whole thing. So that's my first 'Hey I'm doing this in front of other people' memory.

Not only does this memory confirm, for Michael, that he trusted himself as an actor from very early in his life, but it is also a marvellous illustration of what the nineteenth-century poet Samuel Taylor Coleridge called 'the willing suspension of disbelief'. Since this term was coined, it has been used to describe that altered state into which we enter when we are 'lost' in a spectacle of some kind, whether it is a stage play, a movie or a circus. For the moment, we cease to be the logical, practical 'voice of reason' and we become like children again, believing in the magical and the mysterious. For Michael, this suspension of disbelief was crucial to his emotional survival. After the family migrated to New Zealand in 1966, things went from bad to worse:

My parents' relationship got very violent – I remember the worst expression of it was when I was around 14. I had been babysitting my younger brothers since I was nine or ten – a lot of that kind of responsibility, you know? And every time my parents would come home, I would hear them, and wake up and feel this horrible, horrible anxiety and just pray to God that they wouldn't be fighting. Anyway, this one particular night, I remember this terrible fight, and it got so bad, it ended up with me out in the garden at about 3.30 a.m. on a frosty Christchurch morning. I was on the lawn in my pyjamas calling for help. My dad was at the door trying to get me to shut up and my mother was in the kitchen with a broken nose. Finally I came in and my dad tried to hurt me – my mum threw herself between us and he drove off. I was left trying to put my baby brother and my other brother back to bed. It's a terrible thing, you know?

Inside out: becoming an actor

Michael's first memories of escape to that magical world of fantasy were of the Cinerama in Christchurch:

> I'd go there whenever I could, and sit in the front row, and get lost. Sometimes I'd be the only person in the theatre, and I'd sit right in the front row, so I couldn't see the edges, and bang – just get lost … I still like to do that with films.

At school Michael continued to develop the talent for acting that had shown itself so early in his life. He had a friend who was interested in masks and prosthetics – every Saturday they would go and make masks out of plasticine and make home movies with a little 8-mm camera. As a young teenager he also joined a 'Youth for Christ' group, and he recognises that for him this became another way of fostering his own creativity:

> I used to go up to people and say, 'Do you know the Lord Jesus Christ is your personal saviour?' I used to do all that. And the adults could see I could do this, and gave me the responsibility of getting up in front of people at the open air campaigns. In the fourth form, *Jesus Christ Superstar* came out, and I got so moved and upset at hearing the album that I

asked in music class could we do it – and we did it! I directed it and we mimed to the albums and I played Judas, and directed it with all the class. It was a raving success – it was phenomenal!

Michael's trust in himself deepened and was strengthened by his success at school – he won prizes for literature, fencing, public speaking and debating. Although the idea of becoming an actor was not yet formed, he was gathering and consolidating all the resources and skills an actor needs. Also strengthening was Michael's self-reliance, born out of deprivation and lack of support from home. When he was 17, however, the life he had made for himself was badly threatened when his parents sold the family home and returned to England. Michael couldn't stay there – everything that had meaning for him was in New Zealand, so he came back by himself and flatted with some older friends who were students at Auckland University:

I didn't pay rent – I just cooked and did odd jobs – lawn mowing and stuff, and went back to school. I remember feeling like a real Bohemian – these guys were fantastic – books everywhere. That was the other way I escaped – I just read and read. I got right into *The Lord of the Rings* – I mean I did the whole thing – I could speak Elvish!

Yet it seemed that every time he built a world for himself, his parents would demolish it.

My father turned up one day, and he said Mum and the other kids were coming back, and he was leaving, so I'd better go home and look after them. And I had to go and pick up the pieces. It was horrendous. Mum was going to work, but I had the car and I had to drop her off at work every morning, drop the kids off, go to school, pick them up, go home and do the cooking, and then she started going out and getting drunk and going with lots of men. At the end of that year, I was set to go to university and I just said, 'I'm leaving, because if I don't leave now you will never get back on your feet.' And we had this raging, raging argument which she never claimed to remember.

Michael was 19 when he finally managed to break free and begin studying at Auckland University. Shortly after that, he was asked to audition for the Court Theatre, and was taken on as an apprentice. From that point on his career as a stage, television and film actor and director began to take off. He was with the well-known Auckland theatre company Theatre Corporate for seven years, before branching into film and television. In 1993 he was recruited into the cast of the hugely successful *Hercules* series. The character of Iolaus, best friend to Hercules, became enormously popular and on-line fan sites are dedicated to him. Casting Michael in this role was a last-minute decision, based on the intuitive feelings of casting director, Di Rowan. The part had been due to be cast in America, but Di insisted that the directors take a look at Michael. The day after the American directors saw Michael's audition video he was asked to go and talk to them, and a few hours later he was cast in the part. Originally planned as a short-lived character, Iolaus was sentenced to death in episode seven of the first series, but reprieved, brought back to life and went on to become a vital companion to Kevin Sorbo's Hercules. *Hercules* in turn spawned the internationally acclaimed *Xena, Warrior Princess* series, and Michael is looking at a lifetime reputation as something of a cult figure.

Hercules

Looking back on the series now – some 110 hours of television – Michael feels it was an amazing outlet for his physical energy:

> I got to do an awful lot of stuff – running, rolling, riding,
> jumping, falling off things, diving, swimming, fighting,
> climbing, being strapped into things, being hurled from things
> – hugely physical. Really it took care of what I do with my life
> – I was doing that every day – it was fantastic – there was stuff
> to do all the time – every scenario that's ever been done, but
> with a twist – gods and magic!

He also remembers with great affection the friendship he had with Kevin Sorbo, which ran alongside the friendship of Hercules and Iolaus. This reached a crescendo when Kevin returned to shooting after a number of weeks. He had made a valiant recovery from an aneurysm, a serious illness that left him pale, thin and depleted. Michael remembers the day Kevin came back:

> He could only do thirty minutes in front of the camera that
> first day. It was extraordinary – he came back on set looking
> like half the man he was – he did one line and we all burst
> into applause – it was an extraordinary moment.

Such moments of closeness with fellow actors have counted for so much throughout Michael's life, and his days of myth and magic, monsters and gods in *Hercules* seemed to bring him full circle from the little boy who thrust his sword into the belly of the dragon and the distressed child who sat enthralled in the front row of the cinema watching *Ben Hur*.

The place of seeing

Now at the pinnacle of his career, Michael has decided to begin a new venture – a theatre company he calls 'The Large Group'. Their first production was *Hamlet*. Michael talked to me about the trust in his own instinct, his own intuition, that at times has felt almost palpable, and the reciprocal trust that exists between an actor and an audience:

> The audience is trusting me, putting its belief in me –
> receiving a kind of change. Now that's kind of religious for me
> – it's almost like being a high priest. There are a whole lot of
> people in front of you and they're investing all this focused
> energy in you – you become the guide that leads them
> through it all and conducts the change that is made.

Acts of theatre exist in all cultures, and have always been associated with sacred moments of altered states. The word *theatre* comes from the Greek *theatron*, meaning 'the place of seeing'. Inherent to an act of theatre is an audience, a group of witnesses or participants who are there to watch and live through the mysterious stories of other lives. In Ancient Greece, theatre began in 1200 BC as part of the cult of the god Dionysus. The priests of this cult would dance until an altered state was achieved – a state known as 'ecstasis' or ecstasy. In many primitive societies theatre still takes the form of dance and mime, often enacted by medicine men or shamans who are believed to be set apart from ordinary beings, and party to a secret spiritual knowledge of the tribe. Coleridge, in his famous poem 'Kubla Khan', describes it perfectly:

> And all should cry, 'Beware! Beware!
> His flashing eyes, his floating hair!
> Weave a circle round him thrice,
> And close your eyes with holy dread,
> For he on honey-dew hath fed
> And drunk the milk of Paradise.'

The shaman actor lived in a state of trance and vision. Michael Hurst described to me a vision he had, when he was beginning to think about forming The Large Group:

> I had this very clear vision of myself on a very straight, wide path. It was silver in the moonlight, and on either side was very dark, dense bush and trees. It's silver, it's direct, it's straight, it's moonlit – thick forests of stars – and I'm walking up the middle and on either side of the road, directly in line with the edge of my vision, all of these animals are keeping pace with me. Not on the road, on the verge – completely dense, hundreds and hundreds of them, never going in front of me, but keeping exactly in pace with me.

Michael believes that this vision, and other inexplicable feelings he has experienced, are lighting his way ahead. This is where his self-trust is situated – in the area of intuition and instinct. The animals seem to represent that ancient part of him, the part of him that he feels has always been an actor, the part of him that he trusts without question:

> Some things haven't changed for hundreds of years. And that's why I felt the presence of a spirit in me of Hamlet, recognisable to me for the first time as an actual thing, as opposed to an accidental thing. I honestly found myself doing things that I've never been taught to do. There was a moment with Elizabeth Hawthorne (who played Gertrude) in the closet scene, and I was curled up like a little boy whose dad had just gone away, and I found myself pushing her away in a very particular way – and an image flew into my head of some eighteenth-century engraving of Hamlet doing that same thing. I'll be honest – on a couple of nights it felt like someone else was having a go through me. I think I really do believe that – it was amazing. Whatever, wherever it came from, there were some nights when there were transcendent moments …

The actor's inner world

The idea of the actor being possessed is akin to the notion of ecstasy. At the core of what is known as 'method acting' is the belief that the actor gradually becomes the character he is playing, so that ordinary reality ceases to exist. The word 'possession', for most people, conjures up scenes from *The Exorcist* and is coupled with the word 'demonic'. We have it associated with evil and with madness. Yet actors who were trained in the method were taught to open themselves in such a way that the character could enter them fully. I remember sitting in a dressing room with David Suchet, the English theatre, film and television actor (perhaps most famous for his role as Hercule Poirot) as a young actor of 25. He was preparing for a performance of John Aubrey's *Brief Lives*, in which an old man looks back on his life. As David put on layers of make-up and drew in the lines and wrinkles that would one day be etched on his face by age, he gradually became older. It was an extraordinary, almost ghostly experience, watching this young, vigorous man become aged, brittle, with rheumy eyes and drooping lids – his body lost its youth and became bowed and stooping, as if something were sapping him of vitality.

Brian Bates, in his 1986 study *The Way of the Actor*, quotes a similar feeling experienced by film actor Dirk Bogarde, as he prepared for his part in Visconti's award-winning movie *Death in Venice*:

> I started to walk slowly round and round the room, emptying myself of myself, thinking pain and loneliness, bewilderment and age, fear and the terror of dying in solitude. Willing von Aschenbach himself to come towards me and slip into the vacuum I was creating for his presence. He came not all at once, but in little whispers, bringing with him the weight of his years, the irritability of his loneliness, the tiredness of his sick body.

As Brian Bates says, for most of us the idea of possession would be a terrifying thing and we would think we were going mad. Possession has been linked with dissociative identity disorder, a condition made famous by the 1950s movie *The Three Faces of Eve*. We are all aware of different parts of ourselves, sometimes in conflict. One part of us wants to get married, for example, while the other part wishes to remain free and unattached. In the person who suffers from dissociation, however, this split is far more pronounced, so much so that sometimes one part of the personality 'takes over' and obliterates the other part, leaving no memory or awareness. This extreme condition is thought to be caused by extreme trauma in childhood. Children 'escape' to a fantasy world inside their own imagination – a kind of self-hypnosis to help them to survive the worst nightmare.

Dr Jeffrey Mishlove, host of the popular American television series *Thinking Allowed*, is Director of the Intuition Network, an organisation of thousands of individuals in business, government, health, science and education who are interested in cultivating and applying intuitive skills. I wrote to him recently about the discovery I feel I have made in the process of writing this book – that certain people with traumatic childhoods, far from being unable to trust and staying fearful, make a leap into exceptional acts of trust. These people – Rae Evening Earth Ott and her life with wild wolves, Franklin Levinson and his extraordinary communication with horses, Susan Winter with her brave openness to relationships and Michael Hurst as an actor able to achieve true authenticity – seem guided by intuition and by their own sense of true vocation. Dr Mishlove wrote:

> In my own experience, many highly intuitive people (and
> gifted psychics) have experienced childhood trauma. This has
> been confirmed by the research of psychiatrist Colin Ross, of
> Houston, Texas. Children experiencing abusive situations find
> that the physical environment is not safe. They then tend to
> retreat into an inner world. This inner world results in a strong

imaginal life. Psychiatry refers to such a situation as disassociation – meaning that the person detaches from the physical world and develops strong bonds with an interior reality.

What better description could there be of the actor's pursuit of living the life of another? First to imagine, then to become. In *The Way of the Actor* Brian Bates quotes a traditional shamanic actor, talking about an experience of such a 'possession': 'I was obliged, almost without ceasing, to utter loud cries, weep, sing, dance and roll upon the ground … but I was never absent – I always knew what I was saying or doing.'

Bates goes on to say:

> The traditional actor's state of possession is a powerful phenomenon, which alters the actor's behaviour and experience. It is a controlled possession. The traditional actor has a double consciousness; one part is possessed, the other observes and controls.
>
> Theatre director Charles Marowitz points out how, for modern actors, the process of creating a part leads to a trance state very like possession. The actor learns his lines through repetition – this repetition becomes the main preoccupation – the actor continually repeats lines, moods, emotions, situations – he in effect hypnotizes himself. He is still conscious, still aware of everything that is going on around him on the stage and in the auditorium.

Michael described an incident that is a perfect example of such an experience on the stage in his recent role as Hamlet. During the scene known as the 'get thee to a nunnery' scene, Hamlet meets his former sweetheart Ophelia. At this point in the play, Hamlet's mother and his uncle believe he is mad, and Ophelia's father, Polonius, is concealed in the room to eavesdrop on the conversation between Hamlet and Ophelia. Ophelia knows her father is there, and has reluctantly agreed to go along with the 'set up'. Michael described how, in rehearsal, both he and Anna Hewlett (Ophelia) had remained on stage together throughout the scene, yet on one particular night, just at the point where Hamlet realises Polonius is hidden in the room:

> I walked off screaming 'Let the doors be shut upon him!' and I vanished. To Anna's credit she stayed there and was completely as Ophelia would have been, and then the next thing was that I came running back on to say the next line – running out of the darkness, which for her was terrifying and she shrieked. The audience wouldn't have known, but it was all real!

Like traditional shamanic actors, Michael went through a kind of ritual to rid himself of the 'possession' of the character of Hamlet at the end of the production. He went out and danced a lot, and then the next day cut his hair very short. During the rehearsals of *Hamlet*, Michael had had a yearning to do some readings from *Ulysses* by James Joyce.

> I got this overwhelming message in my head saying, 'You have got to do readings of James Joyce on Bloomsday,' which was the Monday after the Saturday we finished *Hamlet*. And I thought – that's too soon – I'm not going to do that. It wouldn't go away – it wouldn't go away – not to put too fine a point on it, I was hearing voices saying 'You must do this'! I'm not mad or anything …

Michael went ahead and booked a local cafe for the Monday evening. At this point he was still unclear about exactly what he wanted to do, but he went with the voices and made a few posters advertising the event. He put the posters up at the cafe and at the university, then he talked to his friend Jason, who had done the music for *Hamlet*, and arranged for musical accompaniment. The evening came, the cafe was packed:

> I was Irish for the whole night. I didn't plan it or rehearse it – I just did it. It was far more out there – far more scary, unknown territory than *Hamlet*. It felt kind of connected to *Hamlet* – a kind of completion and I couldn't explain to you why, but I just knew it was right. And it worked out so well – we all had a marvellous time – we celebrated Bloomsday!

The acorn

In his book *The Soul's Code*, Jungian analyst James Hillman speaks of the 'acorn theory', which holds that each person:

> ... bears a uniqueness that asks to be lived, and that is already present before it can be lived ... a calling may be postponed, avoided, intermittently missed. It may also possess you completely. Whatever – eventually it will out. It makes its claim. The daemon does not go away.

In Greek mythology, daemons were a race of invisible beings. Assigned by Zeus to every mortal, to attend, protect and guide them, they were nameless unless they attended a god or goddess. To live with honour and attend to the voice of intuition is to respect the daemon – to ignore our conscience and our inner world is to go against the daemon. The daemon would die with its assigned mortal, unless the mortal were to become a hero or a champion – every hero who died honourably would ascend to live with the gods. The Romans called it 'genius'; the Christians called it a guardian angel. In Native American myth, it can be a spirit guide in the form of an animal or bird; Jeffrey Mishlove speaks of loving entities, which exist within the imagination of each of us. Whatever the creed, the doctrine or the faith, all human beings aspire – the stronger the link with the inner world, the greater the aspiration. Perhaps the belief in immortality itself is linked with our trust in ourselves.

Michael Hurst has learned to trust his inner world completely, and to let it guide him to fulfilment. It's a kind of surrender. He believes that his intuition will guide him along the silver moonlit path of his vision:

> I've often told younger actors they are capable of feeling every feeling that any human being has ever felt in their lives. In a Jungian sense, we all share in the same emotional and subconscious world – those of us who have the gift of acting can reach into it. That's so real to me, because I do it. When I made that decision, I was open to inspiration, and I trusted that things would come to me, and they have. Before each performance of *Hamlet*, I went and sat in a corner with a very clear channelling crystal, and I just opened myself to the possibilities and the surety of it. I walked on that stage with a comfort and an ease that I always feel on stage. I'm convinced that this is what I've been put here to do.

Perhaps it is this certainty, this heeding of the daemon, that marks out those who truly trust themselves.

Chapter 9

Betrayal and Deception

The dark side of the moon

I have told you many stories of trust – people who trust the animals they love and work with, each other, themselves and the universe in exceptional ways. We can draw much inspiration from the way many people manage to survive the difficulties of their childhood experiences and go on to live fulfilled and creative lives. In this chapter, I am concerned with what happens when trust breaks down, or is deliberately shattered by acts of betrayal and deception. This is the dark side of the moon, that shadowy place where the memories and associations outside of conscious awareness affect our day-to-day dealings with each other. From the moment we enter the world we begin to interact with significant others, and a store of hidden and forbidden feelings begins to build up inside that very personal and mysterious space that has become known as the unconscious.

Archetypes

Since the beginning of time, and in all human cultures, certain symbolic figures have appeared. The influential Swiss psychoanalyst and writer Carl Gustav Jung called these figures 'archetypes'. He believed that these symbols recur because they part of our 'collective unconscious'. In other words, as well as our personal unconscious, which contains all the feelings, memories and associations we have repressed or denied, we also have a set of meanings and symbols that belong to all human beings and can be found in dreams, myths, legends, sculpture, art and music. Jung described these symbols as 'numinous'. The word conveys that which evokes a feeling of intense significance. Numinous images are awe-inspiring and enigmatic. Perhaps one of the most easily recognisable numinous images is the black monolith that appears in the opening scene of Stanley Kubrick's 1968 masterpiece, *2001 – A Space Odyssey*.

One of the first scenes of the film shows prehistoric ape men foraging for food and fleeing their predators. They seem preoccupied with their basic needs and their survival, as one would expect. We see them sleeping in their cave while the sounds of the nocturnal carnivores echo in the dangerous world outside. It is a dark and vulnerable place. In the dawn of the next day, we see something incredible. A black, flawless monolith stands about twelve feet high. It seems to be a form from the future and it hums with magic. Kubrick chose music that reflected the numinosity of the image – Ligeti's 'Requiem' and 'Lux Eterna' (Everlasting Light). The atmosphere is one of sacred awe and significance. We see the ape men amazed by the extraordinary thing that stands in their midst. One of them touches it with great reverence.

Opposite poles

Jung believed that each archetype has within it a force of good and a force of evil. This is clearly shown in the next scene of *2001*. After the ape men have touched the monolith, one of the most famous scenes in cinematic history shows one of the ape men looking at the bone he is holding. As he plays with it and bangs it on the ground, he suddenly understands that the bone can be used as a murder weapon. We see his fist held high, clutching the bone, accompanied by the triumphal music of 'Thus Spake Zarathustra'. From this point on we see the ape men eating meat from the animals they have killed, and killing rival tribes. They are on the way up in terms of evolution. So the force of good within the monolith has advanced humanity – imparted intelligence and understanding – yet the force of bad has allowed power and violence to triumph.

Within all of us are these forces of what we call good and bad. As Shakespeare's Hamlet says: 'Nothing is good or bad but thinking makes it so.' We are brought up to internalise judgements about what is good and what is bad, to be aware of disapproval and to feel shame and guilt about our actions. Dependent on our culture, the intricacies of our various social rules and discriminations will dictate our sense of being a good or a bad person. We are reliant on these rules, to some extent, for our sense of security and trust in ourselves and in each other. Our sense of inclusion in the particular group we belong to is also dependent on knowing what the rules are and having these made explicit to us. As Terry Birchmore writes in his on-line paper 'Shame and Group Psychotherapy':

> Not knowing information that we assume others in the group share disconnects us from group membership. It is a symbol of our inadequacy and unworthiness to be included and to participate. Lack of connection with others is the most shameful of experiences and stirs up Oedipal fears of exclusion and anxieties about our personal worthiness to be accepted and related to as an equal in the group.

Repression

The problem is that this process of shame and exclusion by the powerful members of a group begins when we are too little to understand that there are rules. The small child living as an organism, responding to physical appetites and stimuli, has no idea that there is a rule about where to evacuate its bowel and bladder, no idea that nakedness is acceptable sometimes and not at others, no idea that anger is disturbing and may provoke retaliation. The degree to which adults react to 'transgressions' by the child is directly related to the degree of shame the child experiences, and with shame comes repression. The child who is shamed pushes down feelings that are condemned by the adults around it, and those feelings become disowned. They become a part of the unconscious.

The shadow

Jung was fascinated by the idea of the dark and evil shadow that he believed lurked inside all of us – what he defined in 1945 as 'the thing a person has no wish to be'. He also wrote of two contradictory aspects within the human personality – he referred to them as 'No. 1 and No. 2 personalities'. As a young student, he had a dream during which it seemed he was struggling forwards against a fierce wind in total darkness. There was a fog which further hampered his progress. He had his hands cupped around a tiny light that threatened to go out at any moment. His survival depended on keeping this little light going against all odds. At his back he was aware of a gigantic black figure following him. The atmosphere of the dream was reminiscent of what is perhaps the scariest verse in the history of poetry, from Coleridge's 'The Rime of the Ancient Mariner':

> Like one, that on a lonesome road
> Doth walk in fear and dread,
> And having once turned round, walks on,
> And turns no more his head;
> Because he knows a frightful fiend
> Doth close behind him tread.

Jung interpreted his dream to mean that the little light was his consciousness and the storm, the darkness and the dark giant/fiend who followed him was his unconscious. He believed the shadow inside all of us consisted of the primitive aspects of the mind, those murderous, cruel, enraged, greedy and lustful feelings and impulses that we would prefer to disown and deny.

'Everyone carries a shadow,' Jung wrote, 'and the less embodied it is in the individual's conscious life, the blacker and denser it is.'

As a psychotherapist who specialises in long-term work, I believe that the main task of this work is to help people to come to terms with the shadow self and to bring it from the unconscious into the conscious where it can be recognised and assimilated. It is when the shadow remains locked in the unconscious that it can do most harm. There, it is subject to being 'split off': in other words, we come to believe that we are wholly good and moral beings who would never be capable of ignoble or immoral actions, and from this high ground we see others as wicked and sinful, stupid and greedy. The obsessive dieter who has attained the pared-down elegance of the super-slim looks with disgust at the large person eating a cake. 'How can she be such a pig!' And yet, inside the super-slim woman is a raging longing to gobble cake and chocolate that scares her terribly, and which she keeps at bay like a lion tamer holding a chair against a lion that is threatening to devour him. This longing is denied, stuffed down or repressed, so far down that it becomes inaccessible, and the dieter thinks of herself as pure, good and always in charge of her eating.

At the heart of racism and homophobia, the shadow lurks – it is other people who are debased, stupid, bestial and repulsive. If we separate them from us, as exemplified by the ghastly laws of apartheid that existed in South Africa, then we can occupy our shining moral high ground, having cast the dreadful demons out into the wilderness. But the shadow can also be found in our everyday dealings. We all know people who irk us beyond measure – people who can become an obsessive focus of our frustration and dislike. We may find ourselves replaying certain interactions over and over again. In her paper 'The Shadow', Susan Olson says the shadow has:

… an emotional nature, a kind of autonomy, and accordingly an obsessive quality. If we are feeling unusually emotional about someone or something – if it feels as though our emotions have us rather than our having them – then we might begin to suspect that the shadow is not far from us. If we feel we cannot stand another person, then it's very likely that the other represents significant shadow qualities for us.

The Johari window

Most students of psychotherapy and counselling are familiar with a model called the Johari window. Formulated by psychologists Joseph Lufts and Harry Ingham, it is designed to show different stages of self-awareness in each of us. It is divided into four panes, one open, one closed and two partially closed:

1 open/free area You know Others know	2 blind area Others know You don't know
3 hidden area You know Others don't know	4 unknown area You don't know Others don't know

The first pane represents the open window inside ourselves – the things about us that we know and that other people know: for example, the physical characteristics we have, the job or role we have in the community we live in, all the aspects of ourselves that are evident to others at first meeting. The second pane is the blind area – a one-way pane of glass through which others watch us, but through which we are not able to see. For example, we might think we are very outgoing and confident, but others might perceive us as arrogant and controlling. On a simple level, we might have egg on our faces that others can see but we cannot!

The third pane is the hidden area, a one-way glass in the other direction – all the things we choose to keep secret about ourselves. There can be multiple reasons for this choice – we could be secretive about things we are ashamed of, things we are guarding for fear of being cheated or exposed, things we would simply prefer not to share. This is the area of mistrust, and can also be the area of betrayal and deception.

The fourth pane is the opaque glass through which we 'see darkly' – the unknown area – and it includes everything we do not know about ourselves, and other people don't know either. This could be described as our unconscious – our deep and hidden feelings and motivations that haven't been explored. This is the area we take to psychotherapy, and explore through dream work and feelings that emerge between client and psychotherapist. It is in this area that the shadow lives – indeed, in his later life, Jung asserted that the shadow *was* the unconscious.

Carla and Scarlet

This account of a difficult friendship between two women illustrates how the shadow can lurk in the background of our relationships and result in very painful outcomes.

Carla was a bright, attractive young woman in her early thirties. She had been referred to me by her doctor with terrible post-traumatic stress symptoms resulting from a bereavement, and subsequently, a violent incident. She had been having nightmares and horrifying flashbacks. She shared her life story with a great deal of distress and difficulty.

Carla's mother had been a bossy, controlling woman, the headmistress of the local primary school, a person who enjoyed telling everyone what to do and how to do it. Carla's dad had been an antiques trader – a quiet, solitary and learned person – and Carla had unequivocally adored him. He and Carla had shared a great enthusiasm – antique jewellery. Carla, an only child, had been left completely shocked and alone at 18 years of age, when her parents were tragically killed. (The accident was one of those truly horrible freak events. They had been travelling down a fairly isolated state highway when a truck pulled out in front of them. The driver of the truck had not lived to tell the tale. Carla's parents died at the scene.)

In the years that followed, Carla had 'gone wild'. It was as if she had to get away from her mother's rules and injunctions by doing everything her mother had disapproved of. She spent money 'like water', as her mother would have said: she bought expensive designer denim (her mother hated denim and thought it was 'lower class and common'). Carla adored her flounced denim skirts and jewelled coats. She wore lots of make-up (her mother had often told her she 'looked like a cheap French tart' when Carla put on her black eyeliner and mascara). She slept with several different men.

When she reached the age of 30, Carla had a wake-up call that radically altered her way of behaving. She had gone out to a club and met a very good-looking and seemingly charming guy. In her usual way, she had invited him back to her flat. This time, instead of the usual highly charged evening of playful sex, the night progressed into the worst kind of frightening movie. They had a couple of drinks together, then he began to 'go crazy', calling her all kinds of foul names. He raped her, hit and kicked her, and smashed her beautiful possessions and some precious antiques left to her by her father. She had been sure he was going to kill her. Luckily a neighbour had heard the uproar and called the police. After this incident Carla went through a period of intense fear. She moved out of the city, unable to endure the terrible associations of living in the place where she had been so viciously attacked. She found a timber house out in the countryside about 12 kilometres from the city, where she loved the peace and quiet. She decorated the house exactly as she wanted it and took great care planting and tending a cottage garden. She stayed away from men.

Through her work in psychotherapy, Carla was able to rebuild her sense of inner well-being. She worked on her dreams and her flashbacks. She formed a deep and significant relationship with me, and, in the world outside the therapy room, she began a profitable small business selling jewellery on the internet. She had learned all about antiques from her beloved father and had a good eye for spotting treasures at collectors' markets. She loved walking round suburban neighbourhoods and calling into the local antique dealers, sorting through the trays of gold and silver trinkets looking for bargains.

Gradually her business increased and she opened her own store on the massive American-based auction site, eBay. It was fun! She developed pleasant relationships with her regular customers, writing emails back to them and finding them the exact pendant or locket they had been searching for. She became something of an expert on semi-precious gemstones, particularly the garnets and amethysts she loved. Handling these vibrant deep red and purple jewels gave her a feeling of wholeness and great pleasure. Her jewellery trading was a lifesaver. It meant she could work mostly from home, and when she did go out seeking treasures, it put her in touch with kindly, friendly people and helped her to trust herself and others again. Her eBay trading made her feel that there were good people all over the world who trusted and liked her and who meant her no harm.

Trust in cyberspace

Carla explained the phenomenon of eBay to me. It seems much of it is built on trust. Like a huge department store floating in cyberspace, it rests on the 'feedback' rating of its users. Each trader and customer on eBay (and other internet auction sites) has an individual feedback rating. This is shown as a number after each person's handle name. Users can click on this number and come up with the 'member profile' – a list of comments made by each person who has dealt with them – comments like 'Superb! Brilliant! Very pleased with item and seller!' or, on the negative side: 'Cheat! Thief! Never sent item – don't trust this person!' If there are too many negative comments, the user is suspended from eBay and no longer allowed to use the site. The more positive feedback ratings, the greater the reputation of the user/trader. Carla was proud of her 750 one hundred percent positive feedback rating! She had worked hard for it, carefully choosing and describing each item she sold. She took accurate digital photos of each piece and, when the pieces sold, she enjoyed wrapping them up in violet-coloured tissue and placing them lovingly in small boxes, which she would take great care to label accurately and post off to her customers all over the world.

One of Carla's regular customers lived in Vancouver. Her name was Scarlet. Carla loved dealing with Scarlet – she loved her name, she loved the affectionate emails Scarlet would write to her, and the glowing feedback she would leave for her after each sale was accomplished. Scarlet would often 'buy now', which means that instead of waiting for the auction to finish she would pay the top price that Carla was asking, and pay instantly. Carla and Scarlet began to exchange personal information – the hidden areas in both their lives began to be opened, and they began to self-disclose.

Self-disclosure

Self-disclosure performs several functions in human society. It's a way of gaining information about another person – we start to trust another when we begin to know them. Knowing a person means we can predict their behaviour and responses more reliably. We have an unspoken rule about self-disclosure that is sometimes referred to as 'the norm of reciprocity'. This means that if a person self-discloses to someone else, the other person will self-disclose back. In this way we each build up a store of information about the other person, and this deepens our trust in and understanding of each other.

Carla and Scarlet shared many emails of self-disclosure, at first telling each other about their preferences in clothes and jewellery, then more about their lives so far. It turned out they had both lost their parents fairly early in their lives. Scarlet told Carla her mother had also been killed in an accident when she was 15. Her father, she said, had been a bully and a tyrant and had beaten her up regularly. Carla's heart went out to Scarlet – she knew what that must have felt like! Scarlet had also lived a wild kind of life with lots of boyfriends. She sent Carla a photograph – she was one of those long-haired, long-legged, tanned, gypsy-looking girls that Carla longed to look like (she was small and curvy, with hazel eyes and brown hair). Up to this point, Carla had a very romantic picture of Scarlet in her mind. Scarlet suggested they start to talk on the phone.

Shattered illusions

After a while the phone calls began to be rather onerous for Carla. Scarlet would phone at difficult times – she lived in Canada and Carla lived in New Zealand – and didn't seem to make much allowance for the time difference, ringing Carla too late at night or too early in the morning. Scarlet was also fond of long monologues about herself and her strange beliefs. She was convinced of the existence of extraterrestrials, and went into great detail about what the aliens might look like and where they might be landing. Carla tried to be polite but more and more she felt herself retreating, and she fought against a continual sense of being used as her mother had used her. She found herself resenting the long one-way phone calls. When Scarlet told Carla she was going to be visiting New Zealand as part of a trip to Australia, Carla's heart sank.

Carla felt incapable of saying no to Scarlet and agreed to have her to stay. As the day approached she found herself getting quite excited and told herself that it could be a really good time. She and Scarlet would have fun going to markets together and walking on the beach. Her positive feelings were short-lived, however – when Scarlet appeared at the door, she was not at all what Carla had been expecting. A common problem with internet communication, as most people who use internet dating sites discover, is that the reality very rarely matches up to the image we have created in our minds. The internet provides a perfect arena where we can pretend to be other than we are and assume identities. We can create fantasy selves, and believe in the fantasy selves created by others.

Scarlet had told Carla she was 35, but the woman Carla was now looking at was at least ten years older than that, with a kind of wizened, sunburnt face and long, lank hair – very different from the beautiful photograph she had sent Carla, which must have been taken many years earlier. Carla had prepared a lovely meal, which Scarlet hardly touched. Things went from bad to worse. There was torrential rain that weekend, making it impossible to do much outside. The two women decided to go shopping in the city. On the way there were complicated roadworks and Carla, a nervous driver, had to ask Scarlet to stop talking at her, as she had to concentrate on negotiating her way round the difficult diversions. At this point Scarlet shut her little wrinkled mouth and hardly spoke to Carla again for the rest of the day.

Carla was losing patience. As the wine they had with dinner loosened Scarlet's tongue again, and she started telling Carla about all her different boyfriends, about her experiences with psychic visions and how she could see auras around people, Carla became exasperated. 'What does all this new age stuff mean to you?' she asked irritably. Again, Scarlet became completely silent, and she retired to the bedroom. Early the next morning Scarlet had her bags packed and called the airport shuttle. Carla tried to make amends, feeling she had done something dreadful and been a terrible host. Although she had tried so hard to make Scarlet welcome, she had not been able to endure her.

When Scarlet returned to her home in Vancouver she wrote Carla a series of very nasty emails. She wrote about her own 'spirituality' and accused Carla of being superficial, self-satisfied, materialistic and fat. Carla was mortified. She read and reread the emails time and time again. She went to sleep thinking about Scarlet and burning with indignation. She couldn't believe how much hate and venom Scarlet seemed to feel for her, when before the visit she had seemed so enthusiastic about their friendship. For the past year Scarlet had been sending her gifts and postcards, addressing her with endearments!

Neither of these women had set out to betray or deceive the other, and yet somehow that is exactly how they both ended up feeling. In the absence of face-to-face information, they had become friends in cyberspace. With the first reality check of the phone calls came unease and discomfort, and all illusions were finally shattered as the two women met in person and found that they disliked each other.

The shadow intervenes

Carla told me about a dream she had after Scarlet left:

> I was involved in a cult, all female – living on the banks of a river. I can't remember much about the women – they were a bit like ghosts. Scarlet came to find me and told me of a decision to commit group suicide. She gave me some potion to take, then she disappeared. I swallowed it and then became acutely aware that I only had 24 hours to live. I walked alone by streams, under bridges, and I was starting to

feel the effects of the potion. I had something I had to do (not sure what) and I found my car and started to get into it. I knew I shouldn't drive, that it wouldn't be safe. At this point I felt very relieved. I was sad about dying though.

The dream resonates with the presence of the shadow – represented by the ghostly people and Scarlet, of course. In the dream, the cult could be said to represent a community of women that Carla was trying very hard to belong to. Women are brought up to affirm and flatter each other, to be polite and kind to each other, and to agree with each other. But to have a place in this cult Carla is asked to swallow poison; in other words, to subdue her true feelings. The poison is brought to her by Scarlet. In some ways the poison could be said to represent Scarlet's envy of Carla's obvious advantages. Carla was younger, more financially secure and more psychologically aware than Scarlet. Scarlet implied in her emails that she was superior to Carla, and Carla could have 'swallowed' Scarlet's poisonous remarks and believed that Scarlet was better and more enlightened than her. It was easier to believe that she somehow deserved Scarlet's hate and disgust than to face the real feelings of distaste, disapproval, judgement and dislike that she was experiencing towards Scarlet.

Carla was trying so hard to be unlike her mother, to be sweet, good, kind and generous, to offer and listen and understand, that she was boiling over inside. She had been feeling intense dislike for Scarlet for several weeks before she actually met her, resenting the long, self-involved monologues, secretly ridiculing her for her idiotic beliefs in extraterrestrials, judging her for the bad spelling in her emails. When Scarlet turned up, she had felt very disappointed in the way she looked, and in her taste in clothes. Scarlet was very far from the loving and graceful idealised woman she had imagined. To compensate for these feelings she had felt compelled to keep trying to please Scarlet, but the disappointment and rage kept welling up inside her and wouldn't go away.

The symbol of the car in dreams very often relates to the control we have over our own lives. In Carla's dream, she was in conflict about getting into her car. Should she express her feelings fully, or surrender to the 'cult poison' and give up her true self? She could allow herself to be poisoned by the potion (stay in the hidden and unknown panes of the Johari window) or digest the potion and survive, moving into the open area. To digest the potion would be to come to terms with the previously split-off feelings and accept the angry, disapproving and perhaps cruel part of herself. In the dream, she prefers to die. The child who has been 'used' by the parents for their own needs develops a false self. It is a fantasy of perfection, an ideal self, who never makes mistakes, and never feels ignoble feelings or experiences mean and greedy thoughts. This is how the true self dies, and the false self continues to live on. In Carla's dream, her true self dies, and the false self, who wants to be accepted by 'the cult', will become one of the ghostly cult members.

The false self

As described in a previous chapter, we are all born with an 'organismic self' – in other words, a true set of feelings, preferences and choices that belong to each one of us in an entirely unique way. Jung believed the self was the soul, or the spirit, and that it was the totality of a person's individual being, containing the conscious and the unconscious. He also believed that as we grow we defend the self as we would defend a vault where precious treasure is stored. The more an infant feels attacked by its environment or its caregivers, the stronger its defences are, and the false self serves as a kind of bodyguard. The false self protects the vulnerable self from outer persecution, and also from inner anger and frustration. If a child is badly attacked, in terms of being physically, sexually or emotionally abused, the defences can result in what we now call personality disorders. The narcissistic personality, for example, protects the vulnerable self by building layers of grandiosity and a huge sense of entitlement. Sam Vaknin, an expert on this personality type, and author of *Malignant Self-Love: Narcissism Revisited*, writes in 'The Dual Role of the False Self' (http://samvak.tripod.com):

> The False Self serves as a decoy, it attracts the fire. It is a
> proxy for the True Self. It is tough as nails, and can absorb any
> amount of pain, hurt and negative emotions. By inventing it,
> the child develops immunity to the indifference, manipulation,
> sadism, smothering or exploitation of his parents or other
> primary caregivers. It is a cloak, protecting him, rendering him
> invisible and omnipotent at the same time.

The false self can also become an instrument of betrayal and deception, especially when it is imbued with envy and aggression towards others.

Dearest Jot

The case of the criminal deceptions of the personal assistant at Goldman Sachs who stole 4.5 million pounds was emblazoned over the English newspapers in 2002. Her exploits became compulsive reading – the Cartier jewellery she bought for herself, the Aston Martin Vanquish car she bought for her husband, the villa in Cyprus complete with swimming pool – all the glittering details were devoured by hungry readers like exquisite chocolate treats. Joyti de Laurey began working for Goldman Sachs (dubbed Golden Sachs by the newspapers) in 1998. Before that she had narrowly avoided bankruptcy when her sandwich shop in East London went out of business. Joyti was a well-educated, well-spoken, intelligent and creative Indian woman with a large, curvaceous body and a discreet warmth. She also appeared to be extremely reliable, and very hard working.

Jennifer Moses, an executive director in mergers and acquisitions at Goldman Sachs, and her husband Ron Beller, a fixed income trader, took Joyti on as their personal assistant. 'Dearest Jot', as Jennifer Moses was later to refer to her, became indispensable to the fabulously wealthy couple. In June 2001 Ron Beller asked Joyti to arrange a surprise fortieth birthday party for Jennifer in Rome. The three-day celebration began with champagne and canapés for 40 couples before continuing on to dinner and dancing at the exclusive club La Dolce Vita. The following morning guests were chauffeured to a lavish all-day party at a Roman castle. The finale was a superb brunch at an Italian villa, while a string quartet played for the guests. Joyti was among the guests, and toasted Jennifer Moses in glowing terms. Back in London, Jennifer wrote Joyti a note, with which she enclosed a gift of expensive jewellery and a cheque for £5000. 'Dearest Jot,' she wrote, 'this just gilds the lily, but it's a way of saying thank you for the best weekend of my life. Your toast will always be etched on my heart. You are truly amazing.'

Joyti lived almost entirely in the hidden area of the Johari window. Her false self was the only one known to others. For while she was acting as the perfect, adoring, loyal and trustworthy personal assistant to Jennifer and Ron, she was forging their signatures on the chequebooks with which they had trusted her. To cover her theft, she replenished the cash in the couple's British cheque account with money she transferred from their accounts at the bank's 'wealth management unit' in New York. It seems that Jennifer and Ron suspected nothing, but at some point in 2001 Jennifer asked Joyti to draw up a list of their expenditure. Joyti didn't carry out this request, but told Jennifer the birthday party had been very costly, and that was why their expenses seemed higher than usual.

Joyti's deception extended beyond the financial. She had formed what seemed to be a personal and close friendship with Jennifer

Moses. In November 2000 she told Jennifer that her husband was having an affair and she wanted to move out and get a house for herself and her son. Jennifer lent Joyti £40,000 interest free so that she could do this – Joyti repaid the loan from the couple's own money, which she had stolen from their accounts. She told Jennifer she was suffering from cervical cancer, which was untrue. Jennifer was deeply affected by this as her own mother had been fighting cancer for some months. She offered to pay for Joyti's treatment in New York. Dearest Jot used the money to have a five-star vacation at the Peninsula Beverly Hills Hotel and to spend vast sums in the surrounding boutiques.

When Moses and Beller retired from Goldman Sachs in 2001, Joyti went on to forge cheques and steal from the accounts of her new boss, investment banker and multi-millionaire Scott Mead. In 2002, after Scott Mead had decided to add an apartment in New York to his growing collection of homes, Joyti realised it would be the perfect cover for her single largest theft. Her regular contact with the private wealth management team who looked after the investments of Goldman Sachs' top executives, and the trust that she engendered in all who dealt with her, made her fraud easy. After casually informing one of the team that the apartment's vendor lived in Cyprus, she forged Mead's signature on an authentic-looking transfer request and asked for the £2.25 million to be sent to an account in Cyprus in the name of J. Schahhou (Joyti's maiden name).

Between February and April 2002 she pocketed a further £1.1 million. On May 1, Scott Mead asked the wealth management team to make a sizeable donation to Harvard, his former college. He was shocked to learn that he did not have enough money remaining in his account, and furthermore, that unauthorised transfers had been made to Cyprus. By that time Joyti had handed in her notice, telling Mead she was moving to Cyprus as the Archbishop of Nicosia's new assistant. Scott Mead called in the head of security, and the next day Joyti was arrested. She has since been sentenced and is now in jail in the UK.

Letters to God

Joyti's false self seems to have been fragmented into two parts. There was the facade of a compliant and discreet servant, and running alongside, a huge sense of entitlement to all the advantages and riches of her bosses. As Sam Vaknin says: 'The narcissist is saying, in effect: "I am not who you think I am. I deserve a better, painless, more considerate treatment." ' This sense of entitlement makes itself very evident in the most bizarre feature of the Joyti de Laurey case. In a couple of notebooks that she called her 'Bible of Daily Thoughts', Joyti wrote strange child-like little letters to God. It is a striking example of the false self protecting the true self: she asks God for protection as if he is truly listening to her and accepting her, and as if he should indulge her criminal activities and allow her to escape undetected with all her pilfered loot:

> Dear God, I don't want to lose Jen's trust over anything. Please protect me. I have only to secure another 40 [thousand] and I'm done. Please ensure they haven't discovered anything. I need to be alright. So much is depending on me – the car, the house, etc, etc. I just want everything to be fine. Please, please God, ensure my relationship with Jen is untarnished. With nothing but all my heart, J.

On another occasion, she wrote:

> Dear God, I write to you worried and fearful that once again I could find myself in serious trouble. Please protect me. I need one more helping of what's mine and then I must cut down and cease in time all the plundering.

During her three-month trial, Joyti claimed that transfers to her account had been legitimate payment for helping the three Goldman bosses run their private lives and conceal extramarital affairs. She fought the charges of theft and fraud vigorously, and appeared 'tough as nails' and without emotion in court. The vulnerable little child who had written to God (or appealed to the false self to cover her shame) – 'Why do I get so scared? What will become of me? Please look after me and keep me and my family safe and without money worries ...' – was banished back into her private hell, and in its place was the glittering veneer. Joyti and her lawyers claimed the stolen money was a 'reward for being me'.

Surely that is what every child deserves – a rewarding life just for being themselves – unconditional love, acceptance and regard. We must assume that Joyti was severely deprived of these childhood rewards, and that the bitterness, anger, envy and resentment was stored up inside her until she was given the opportunity to release it.

The archetypes of success

As humanity has advanced in terms of invention and achievement, so the numinous images of our civilisation have become more and more linked with material success. Joyti coveted the possessions and outward symbols of success that her employers enjoyed – the cars, the jewellery and the overseas villas. These possessions become linked to a feeling of being chosen, being significant, being special. The face of a supermodel; the brand new, shining car; the silks and satins of a designer ballgown; the vase of immaculate flowers in the ideal home – all of these images are imbued with feelings of sacred significance as we become more and more likely to worship material perfection rather than spiritual enlightenment. But inside the archetype of perfect beauty lurks the two-headed beast of envy and greed.

Ripley

We want our villains to be charming and beautiful – we want them to represent our envy and greed inside a beautiful exterior. We want them to act out for us our most heinous desires. A vast percentage of the most popular books and movies involve scams, heists, counterfeit, fraud and 'stings'. We love to witness criminals at work – especially if they are attractive, clever criminals. We want them to escape – our hearts pound for them when they are evading capture and we long for them to be on the boat or the plane, enjoying the blue sea and the sunshine, having successfully evaded the police with their ill-gotten gains. Perhaps the most disturbing of these stories is Patricia Highsmith's brilliant study of the poor orphaned boy who becomes a consummate trickster, *The Talented Mr Ripley* (made into a compelling film by Anthony Minghella).

We are introduced to Tom Ripley as a harmless beast who skulks around thinking up cheap scams. Like a marauding wild animal in a city full of humans, he lives in fear of entrapment. He is being followed by a man called Greenleaf, a desperate father from the upper echelons of New York society who wants Tom's help to find his son, Dickie. Ironically, Tom's name has surfaced through some friends of Dickie's who remembered how clever and helpful Tom had been when they got in a muddle with their income tax. 'Charley could have told Mr Greenleaf that Tom was intelligent, level-headed, scrupulously honest and very willing to do a favour. It was a slight error.'

But Mr Greenleaf is completely taken in as Tom's adrenalin surges and his performance as a helpful, jolly decent young man, who has been a really close and good friend to Dickie, gathers momentum. His mind whirrs like a machine assessing and measuring his opportunities to exploit and deceive. He realises that Herbert is presenting him with such an opportunity: 'Tom's heart took a sudden leap. He put on an expression of reflection. It was a possibility. Something in him had smelt it out and leapt at it even before his brain.' Greenleaf hires Tom to go to Italy, to the small fishing village where Dickie now lives, and his brief is to persuade Dickie to come back home.

Tom slides into different identities as smoothly as a chameleon's tongue darts out and rolls up the unsuspecting fly. On the boat to France he plays the part of the wealthy, aloof, serious young American with something very important to do. Once in Mongibello, where Dickie is leading a very pleasant life with a young woman called Marge, Tom glides into his role as Dickie's best friend, enjoying every moment of the lifestyle, food, wine and travel that such a position affords. It all goes very well for some weeks. People trust Tom easily – he has a kind of anonymity – he has 'the world's dullest face, a thoroughly forgettable face', and a formidable talent for imitating the manners and style of whomever he finds himself with. However, Dickie and Marge start to tire of Tom. For a while, Tom had felt convinced that he was as significant to Dickie as Dickie was to him. When it eventually becomes apparent that Dickie is getting bored and uncomfortable with him, Tom decides to exterminate him and it is almost as though he has decided to smash a mirror that is no longer offering a good reflection:

> He wanted to kill Dickie. It was not the first time he had thought of it. Before, once, twice or three times, it had been an impulse caused by anger, or disappointment, an impulse that had vanished immediately and left him with a feeling of shame. Now he thought about it for an entire minute, two minutes, because he was leaving Dickie anyway, and what was there to be ashamed of any more? He had failed with Dickie, in every way. He hated Dickie … he had offered Dickie friendship, companionship, and respect, everything he had to offer, and Dickie had replied with ingratitude, and now hostility. Dickie was shoving him out in the cold. If he killed him on this trip, Tom thought, he could simply say some accident had happened. He could – he had just thought of

something brilliant: he could become Dickie Greenleaf himself!

And so he does. Dickie becomes yet another version of Tom's false self. Assuming Dickie's identity more or less completely, Tom seems to have not a moment's remorse or regret for smashing his friend's skull with an oar and, weighting the body down, pushing him overboard like an unwanted piece of luggage. On the contrary, he feels an 'ecstatic moment' when, travelling away from the scene of the crime, he thinks of Dickie's money, the travel, the luxury, the beautiful clothes, freedom and pleasure that he can now enjoy. He is completely confident in his cold-blooded planning. Tom goes on to kill another young man who threatens his new identity as Dickie. Again he is remorseless and compassionless, murdering Freddie brutally and disposing of the body with a little irritation at its heaviness but no feeling of shame or guilt. Tom continues to enjoy Dickie's stolen identity and lifestyle as the book progresses. Despite brushes with the police and Dickie's concerned family and friends, Tom evades capture with consummate grace and ease, and on the last page we see him intent on heading for Crete and a life of luxury. In his pocket is a grateful letter from Mr Greenleaf informing him that he has inherited Dickie's trust fund and possessions.

Inside the psychopath

Tom is a classic example of a psychopath. We know that he was orphaned when he was very young, and raised by an unempathic aunt who treated him as an unpleasant burden. Unable to feel any closeness with anyone, he is also incapable of warmth, love and empathy. There simply is no true self in the psychopath. The false self feels omnipotent, superb – ten feet tall and bullet-proof. There often seems no vulnerability or shame at all. The psychopath simply glides around the world using, abusing and even murdering people with no feelings whatever. Tom is a total isolate, living almost completely in his imagination – occasional feelings of fear of entrapment lurk in the innermost recesses of his mind, but absolutely no remorse.

The usual history of the psychopathic personality is that there has been no consistency in the parenting. Often lacking a stable, loving background, the psychopath has been unable to take in any 'good object' – in other words, the loving presence and encouragement of an involved caregiver has been absent, and so the child learns nothing about closeness, containment and intimacy. Learning to rely on native wit, the psychopath is a survivor with an intense motivation to succeed. Perhaps the most chilling passage in *The Talented Mr Ripley* is the description towards the end of the book of Tom's inner picture of killing Dickie's girlfriend Marge. His plan has almost reached its culmination – he has managed to convince everyone and escape detection for his impersonation of Dickie and the two murders – when Marge discovers Dickie's rings in a box and confronts Tom with them:

He was holding the shoe in both hands in a position to use the wooden heel of it as a weapon. And how he would do it quickly went through his head: hit her with the shoe, then haul her out by the front door and drop her into the canal. He'd say she'd fallen, slipped on the moss.

Mr Ripley and Patricia Highsmith

Patricia Highsmith's intense connection with the character of Ripley has been a subject of fascination among critics and film directors. When she was plotting the novel in 1954, she wrote: 'In Tom Ripley, I am showing the unequivocal triumph of evil over good, and rejoicing in it. I shall make my readers rejoice in it too.'

She went on to write four other Ripley novels, and began to sign letters and dedications to friends as 'Tom (Pat)' and 'Pat H alias Ripley'. When *The Talented Mr Ripley* won the Edgar Allan Poe award in 1956, Pat altered the inscription on the certificate to read 'Mr Ripley and Patricia Highsmith'. She later said she thought he deserved the honour as much as her: 'I often had the feeling Ripley was writing it and I was merely typing,' she said. In another incident, the artist Peter Thomson, a fellow resident of the Italian village of Positano, where Highsmith lived for a long time, remembers that she walked up to him and said, 'You remind me of Tom Ripley.' He said it was as if she was speaking of someone she knew. As Andrew Wilson says in his biography of Highsmith, *Beautiful Shadow*: 'Knew him she did, for Ripley was an embodiment of her creative imagination at work, a representation of her unconscious and a shadowy symbol of her repressed, forbidden and occasionally quite violent desires.'

Like Ripley, Patricia Highsmith had grown up as an unhappy and isolated child. Nine days before her birth, her parents divorced. Her mother remarried when Pat was three, and the child never liked her stepfather. Moving between Texas and New York, Pat's mother was continually at odds with her second husband, and when Pat was 12 she was left with her grandmother in Fort Worth while her mother and stepfather had yet another reconciliation. She felt lonely and abandoned. In her teens she began writing her disturbing stories, shaping her unhappiness into words in a quest, as she later wrote, 'for order and security'. These qualities were easier for her to find in books than in real life. She was alienated, and confused about her longings for same-sex relationships.

Fascinated by matters of good and evil, morality and immorality, Patricia Highsmith wrote some of the most disturbing fiction of the twentieth century. 'You're sort of at sea in her books,' wrote her publisher Otto Penzler; 'you don't know who are the bad guys and who are the good guys, because there are no nice people. Nobody's nice, nobody's good.' There are many parallels between Patricia's life as a writer and Ripley's life of the imagination. In his extreme inner isolation Ripley invents, imagines scenarios, composes speeches and letters. His assumption of Dickie's identity can be compared with the vicarious lives that a writer such as Highsmith lives through her characters. As Wilson says:

> When Ripley is forced to step back into his own self in the final chapter, he is, like a novelist who has fallen in love with her protagonist, utterly miserable. After all, being oneself again was so boring after the excitement and drama of pretending to be another.

Perhaps the thing Patricia longed for was to express all the emotions she had been forced to repress. Only then might she live, like Ripley, without shame in a universe that would allow her to escape recrimination and judgement, and take off, all alone, as he does, for an unencumbered life of luxury.

Heart of stone

Sam Vaknin sees our fascination with evil and the amoral as having other facets. Not just a feature of our repressed desires, evil has always been linked with power and status: 'A heart of stone lasts longer than its carnal counterpart,' writes Sam. 'Throughout human history, ferocity, mercilessness and lack of empathy have been extolled as virtues and enshrined in social institutions such as the army and the courts.' Sam also sees it as a feature of our arousal/sensation-seeking society – we crave stories about deceivers and betrayers, murderers and rapists, the Hannibal Lecters, Joyti de Laureys and Tom Ripleys of the world, to:

> ... enliven our gossip, colour our drab routines and extract us from dreary existence – a little like collective self-injury. Self-

mutilators report that parting their flesh with razor blades makes them feel alive and reawakened. In this synthetic universe of ours, evil and gore permit us to get in touch with real, raw, painful life.

Perhaps we are also attracted to the 'hard as nails' false self because we fear the pain of connecting with our vulnerable core. One of the connections between the betrayers and deceivers Joyti de Laurey and Tom Ripley is that they both kept secret and hidden their vulnerable selves, and they were both incapable of any true closeness. It is this vulnerable core that allows us to be involved in truly close and intimate relationships and to know the joy – and anguish – of love.

Kill Bill

In the virtuoso comic book films *Kill Bill Volume 1* and *Kill Bill Volume 2*, the legendary film-maker Quentin Tarantino tells the story of The Bride, aka Black Mamba aka Beatrix Kiddo aka Mommy. Played by delicate blonde actress Uma Thurman, the innocent, pregnant, fairy-like bride becomes a samurai sword-wielding, kung fu master. She storms through the film slicing off arms and heads, ripping out eyeballs and hearts. Although the reasons for her fury are complex, the main motive appears to be revenge. She will kill Bill, her former partner, for all his acts of betrayal, not least of which is beating her almost to death on her wedding day.

Like one of the Furies in Greek mythology, the Bride is an avenging superhuman being who survives trauma and attack like a goddess. The Furies had long hair made of snakes, and their eyes dripped with blood. We see the Bride mangled, bleeding, dying and buried alive. One of her aliases is Black Mamba – the most poisonous snake in the world. Yet the Furies were not just rebellious women. They fought for law and order and hounded criminals to their death. So, the criminal

Bill is hounded by the Bride. We see her being schooled by the merciless and inhuman kung fu master Pai Mei. His heart is decidedly one of stone, and he helps the Bride to forget Beatrix Kiddo, the child she once was, and turn her own heart into stone too. She can cut through solid wood with her bare hand, burst out of sealed coffins, take on any adversary, gouge out eyes and slice off body parts without the least flicker of emotion. She is able to avenge herself on all those who threaten her, until the finale, when, armed with a sword and her stone heart, she tracks down Bill to his lair.

Instead of the sordid bar or trailer we expect, Bill's lair turns out to be an elegant, ordered house in California where he has been concealing his secret weapon – a beautiful four-year-old child. Bill is the little girl's father and her mother is the Bride, who deserted her baby long ago. A remarkably civilised and low-key scene follows, during which the Bride, now Mommy, makes friends with her child, and Bill and Mommy both tend to her. But Mommy still has to kill Daddy, because he deserves to die. The final coup is the Mommy's delivery of the 'five point palm exploding heart technique'. Touching five pressure points taught to her by Pai Mei, Mommy causes Bill's heart to explode. We must assume his heart has not been turned to stone. They are both vulnerable human beings after all! Mommy claims Baby and, as the film ends, we see her lying on the floor, laughing and crying – overcome by all the emotion she has previously repressed.

The power of love

The couples that I see in the therapy room are all too often occupying that same battleground – albeit in less dramatic fashion – as Bill and Mommy. Each feels betrayed by the other, each wants revenge. Very often there have been incidents of deceit, lying and concealing. The 'wounded partner' finds it impossible to forgive, blames the other unequivocally and feels compelled to stay in the lofty ground of unyielding righteousness. The partner who has been guilty of deception often blames the other for a catalogue of faults and feels justified in the misdemeanours. Hurt is a danger zone, because to admit hurt is to become vulnerable, so the stone heart prevails. It seems to me that unless we can connect fully to our own humanity, our vulnerability and our fallibility, we will stay locked in the fight. It is only when the Bride can accept the little girl she has denied and abandoned that she can become a human being and not a Fury. Love hurts, says the old song, but without love we have nothing. If we are incapable of intimacy and closeness we live lives of emptiness and inner isolation. The stone heart may last longer than its carnal counterpart, but like a marble statue, it is inanimate, cold and dead.

Conclusion

Thorns and roses

When King Lear asks his daughters for affirmations of love so that he can decide how to divide his kingdom between them, he makes a mistake that can never be put right. Love cannot be put into words – the daughter who loves him the most, Cordelia, says: 'Unhappy as I am, I cannot heave my heart into my mouth!' At this stage Lear can only trust the outward appearance and expression of love. The two daughters who flatter and pander to him with their wonderful speeches of adoration gain his approval and his legacy of wealth and riches. He has still to understand that real love between human beings is an on-going journey which can involve great pain, tribulation and difficulty, and that trust must be the foundation stone of that love.

In 'The Thorn upon the Rose', Mary Black sings:

Don't forget the thorn upon the rose!
Its cut is deep, and the scar lasts forever:
It follows love wherever love goes.

We all learn by experience. Babies reach out for the roses of love with no thought or concept of the thorn. They do not expect to be hurt. They cry when they feel something unpleasant – a cold draught, a pain in the tummy, a sharp pin – but they do not expect to be hurt. Children, like little sponges, absorb the ways of their parents, their siblings, their environment. They absorb ideas expressed by older children and adults around them.

We all know how hard it is to refrain from swearing when a little three-year-old is around, knowing how our words will emerge enthusiastically from her mouth. I remember my son coming home from school when he was just five years old and announcing to me: 'You're a bad person if you don't believe in Jesus!' I was horrified at the assurance with which he delivered this statement, and over several days gently explained to him that many cultures existed and that people have different beliefs, different names for their gods, and that perhaps bad people might be those who deliberately set out to hurt another person or animal. Children learn, then, from us. The baby looks at its mother and then its father with total trust, total dependence and utter reliance. As the baby grows into a child, it starts to internalise the behaviour and beliefs of those significant others at home and at school.

Erikson and the stages of identity

The psychoanalyst Erik Erikson had a particular interest in the development of children and adolescents. He studied the Oglala Lakota Native Americans, his research following the tribal tradition whereby the boy, at puberty, was sent on a search for a spirit guide. Alone and without weapons, food or clothes, the boy would wander in the woods until a dream came to him of an animal or bird. This creature would then be revealed to tribal elders, who would interpret the boy's future path. The animal or bird would define whether the boy was to become a medicine man, a hunter, a maker of weapons or a priest. In our society, children wander lost in the maze of choices that confront them in their search for meaning, depending on their own sense of identity and whatever help they might gather from the adults in their lives.

In the theory of psychosocial development he describes in *Childhood and Society*, Erikson writes of eight separate stages in the development of our identities – the sense we have of who we are and how we define ourselves as separate and unique human beings. To complete each stage positively is to be able to move on successfully to the next. The first stage, which lasts from birth to one year, Erikson calls 'Trust versus Mistrust'. From the moment of birth, children begin to learn the ability to trust others based on the calm and containing consistency of their caregivers. If trust develops successfully, the child develops confidence and security and does not feel threatened by the world around. If the caregivers are inconsistent and unpredictable or, worse still, aggressive to the growing baby, then the result is that the child will be anxious, hyperalert and fearful and will find it difficult to relax. Such a child will begin to expect that all flowers have thorns.

The next stage is 'Autonomy versus Shame and Doubt'. Between the ages of one and three, children begin to move towards independence. They begin to say no, to make choices and decisions based on their own wishes. If children are encouraged and supported in this new-found independence they become more confident and secure in the world. If they are criticised and over-controlled, if the caregiver is fearful or hostile to their growing wish to assert themselves, then they start to feel inadequate and lack self esteem, relying on the opinions and wishes of others to guide them. This child will not trust himself to find the thornless flowers, but rather will continually ask others which is which.

The third stage, 'Initiative versus Guilt', describes the years between three and six, when children love to play make-believe games and initiate activities with others. Houses are made of blankets, spaceships exist in a cardboard box; princesses and aliens, monsters and heroes are enacted and enjoyed with a joyful enthusiasm. In this stage, intuition and creativity can develop and blossom into a rose of intense colour. Thorns, at this stage, can be accepted as part of the whole, and if the child has faith, she can deal with them. This is the stage when good kindergarten or primary school teachers can help the child towards a trust in the environment even if that trust is unavailable at home. Conversely, if the fragile petals of these inner flowers are trampled on with contempt, irritability or impatience, the child can learn to feel like a nuisance to others and lose the impetus to trust in his own creative impulses. The rose seems nothing but thorns.

The fourth stage, 'Industry versus Inferiority', lasts from the age of six to puberty. Children develop pride in their accomplishments, they see projects through and feel good about what they achieve. In this stage also, teachers can have a huge impact on the growing selfhood of the child. If children are reinforced and encouraged in their attempts, if success is not overemphasised, they develop a strong sense of their ability to achieve and complete things. If, however, teachers have a rigid idea of a standard that has to be reached and are overcritical at this stage, children can rapidly lose heart and feelings of inferiority can cause depression and dejection, even despair. Thorns can attack the child from inside at this stage, with inner torments of self-criticism taking over from the external critics.

In adolescence, 'Identity versus Role Confusion' is the stage to navigate. Potential young adults begin to contemplate their future, decide on their preferences in appearance, self-presentation, sports, careers and partners. They explore and form their identities depending on the outcome of their exploration. Roses can be huge and scarlet at this time of life, shocking and challenging, provoking a reaction. If the reaction is one of ridicule, contempt or hostility, the large scarlet rose can wither on its stem – identity can be stifled and in its place comes confusion and searching, which in turn can result in self-destructive or reckless behaviour. Internal thorns can rip the self to shreds.

In young adulthood, we reach the stage of 'Intimacy versus Isolation'. We look outside the family for love and closeness. We look for a soulmate. If relationships within the family have been traumatic, most of us hope for reparative experiences with a partner. The hope is still alive inside us that we might find that special person who will celebrate our existence. Simon and Garfunkel's famous song 'Bridge over Troubled Water' says it all for most of us at this stage – this is what we long to hear:

When tears are in your eyes, I will dry them all –
I'm on your side – when times get rough
And pain is all around,
Like a bridge over troubled water
I will lay me down.

It's a big ask. Many of us are dreadfully let down and disappointed when that special other cannot provide the care and selfless generosity for which we hunger. Worse still, if the chosen partner doesn't respond to our love at all, and instead repeats the rejection we have already experienced, then we retreat into wounded isolation, this time even more certain that we are unlovable. If this is the conclusion we reach, then there are no more flowers, for the thorns have entered our hearts.

The immortal spirit

Dust as we are, the Immortal Spirit grows
Like Harmony in Music ...

William Wordsworth wrote these inspiring words in 'The Prelude' over two hundred years ago – I believe that what he meant was that we have within us the capacity to grow, heal and create no matter what we have been through. The concept of the soul or spirit is universal and cross-cultural – whatever our religion or political persuasion, wherever we were born and educated, most of us human beings have a feeling that part of us will survive death in some form. Certainly we seem to have the innate ability to survive damage and trauma in our lifetimes through our own intuition, strength and creativity.

At the crucial stage of developing her identity, Rae Evening Earth Ott found her surrogate father, Snow Eagle:

With Snow Eagle, I wiped my slate clean and began a

relationship that taught me trust through deeds and a spiritual connection. I was encouraged to make mistakes and taught to embrace them. In my mind and heart and spirit, this man was and always will be, my true father. In our culture, adoption is final and forever. I was loved and cared for as if I'd grown up with him. Under his careful tutelage, I opened up and began a journey into myself.

At the same stage, searching for an identity, Franklin Levinson found Rowena:

> She helped me begin to know that I was good, I deserved to have some peace and love in my life, and I didn't have to be something other than who I was naturally. I am now 55 years of age: she passed away two years ago. We remained extremely close throughout our lives from the time we met. Rowena was the first free spirit I ever met. The first person to whom love was more important than a bank account or how things looked to the neighbours. The first person I ever met who made peace and love a priority in their life … thank you Rowena …

At the later stage of intimacy versus isolation, Susan Winter found a beautiful first love with a younger man:

> I totally trusted him, with all my heart. If I were away all day on business in NYC, I knew that if he'd been in a room full of Playboy bunnies, he'd just have waited for me to return. He was honest in his communications, so I had no reason to wonder as to his real meaning. He truly loved me. I knew it and felt it. This 'boy's love' was pure and honest. It was unedited and flowed freely. We were able to release our past and trust each other. We were gentle and understanding.

At this same stage, Duncan found the relationship he had been waiting for with Andrew:

> For the past three years, I have been enjoying the most wonderful, loving, honest and caring relationship of my life. I met him in a bar – we went back to my place and spent the next four or five hours talking. It was one of those moments you read about in romance novels, where you know you have met Mr Right! Something strange and new had happened – it was the first time in my life that I had let down the barriers, and decided to be me. Just me. More importantly, it was the first time in my life that I could honestly say that I loved myself. Not in an arrogant way, but accepting myself and appreciating who I am on every level, without criticism or judgement. A person who is worthy of receiving love.

Not expecting Andrew to sacrifice himself and keep on giving, Duncan has reached a mature perspective on how the relationship works:

> At the time I met Andrew, I no longer needed other people's approval to live my life. Because of this, I am able to trust his love and really enjoy it without worrying and fearing it may be taken away. On the night we first met, one of the things we agreed about is how much we both hated the expression 'my other half'. Andrew is not my other half, nor I his. We are whole individuals.

At 40, just at the time when things were at their worst and her sister was dying of cancer, Tammy found Annie: 'Mentally I was a wreck, and she was my knight in shining armour. She just made me feel better about myself and that I didn't have to be a prostitute – I didn't feel dirty any more.'

As a small child, Michael Hurst found teachers fostering his talent and creativity and reinforcing his ability. The nuns who picked him out to show how St George killed that dragon gave him the opportunity to believe he was special; the secondary school teachers who worked with him on *Jesus Christ Superstar* and believed in him as a director and actor encouraged him to grow spiritually through a troubled adolescence. Later, Michael's identity as an actor grew stronger as others saw the bright flame of his gift shining out in the darkness – he was chosen. Then, too, there was the feeling of being part of a community, which is still life-enhancing for Michael:

> Especially with the theatre, what you are doing is giving – you're giving to an audience and giving to the other actors. When I'm directing, I tell actors, 'You have a right to ask for what you want from another actor, but only if you're giving it.' You can't act in isolation. It's very real. It's the same with Jennifer, my wife – she's incredibly practical. You know it's very real – our lives are very real.

Knowing ourselves, loving others

This is trust – to know ourselves as fully as we can. Perhaps this, above all, is the message of the Fool to King Lear – know yourself well enough to trust yourself and your own judgement. Erikson's last two stages – 'Generativity versus Stagnation' and 'Ego Integrity versus Despair' – are those we reach in middle and old age, when we are coming to terms with the meaning of life and the inevitability of death. Generativity is the ability to love and care for the future generations. The roses are still blooming and at this stage we can accept the thorns as a vital part of the mature rose bush. Stagnation, on the other hand, is self-absorption – still searching for gratification from others. Stagnant roses smell worse than weeds and their thorns are poisonous.

King Lear, at the start of the play, personifies this self-involved quest for affirmation. He bases his trust for his daughters on their ability to flatter him. He has no intrinsic belief in himself. He is unable to generate love for anyone else. He would not know how to handle a wolf, soothe a horse, choose a lover or a friend. When he is rejected, he feels absolute despair. It is only when he has undertaken his journey to emotional maturity through his time of suffering out on the wild moor that he comes to know himself, to achieve integrity within himself and to value the truth and loyalty of his daughter Cordelia, who was unable to 'heave her heart into her mouth' and put into words her deep love for her father. Over her dead body, Lear finally comes to recognise that reciprocity of love is the most important thing in our lives.

Unless we can somehow surmount the trauma and difficulty we might experience during our lives (often by finding a replacement parent or parental figure), we can never trust ourselves, and therefore never trust another being – animal or human. The trust our children place in us, their loved adults, is the greatest trust of all. Honouring that trust by nurturing, encouraging, protecting, accepting, respecting and believing in our children is the most important task we undertake. This book is a testament to the impact of childhood on our capacity to trust and our ability to live and love. By understanding and healing ourselves, we can plant the seeds of love, faith, trust and hope in the fertile ground of our children's lives and watch those seeds come to a resplendent and joyful flowering in the gardens of their future.

Bibliography

Books and papers

Bates, Brian, *The Way of the Actor*, Century, 1986.

Bettelheim, Bruno, *The Uses of Enchantment*, Penguin, 1976.

Brings, Felicia and Winter, Susan, *Older Women/Younger Men: New Options for Love and Romance*, New Horizon, 2000.

Browning, Frank, *A Queer Geography*, Noonday, 1996.

Campbell, J.K., *Honour and the Devil*, Oxford, 1965.

Coetzee, J.M., *Disgrace*, Vintage, 2000.

Collins, Billy, *Taking Off Emily Dickinson's Clothes*, Picador, 2000.

Dickinson, Emily, *Selected Poems*, Bloomsbury Poetry Classics, 1992.

Dowrick, Stephanie, *Forgiveness and Other Acts of Love*, Viking, 1997.

Erikson, Erik, *Childhood and Society*, W.W. Norton, 1993.

F., Christiane, trans. Susanne Flatauer, *Autobiography of a Street Girl and Heroin Addict*, Bantam, 1982.

Fone, Byrne, *Homophobia*: A History, Metropolitan, 2000.

Forster, E.M., *Howards End*, Penguin Signet Classics, 1998.

Freud, Sigmund, *Introductory Lectures on Psychoanalysis*, Penguin, 1973.

Friday, Nancy, *Men in Love*, Arrow, 1980.

Gabbard, Glen, *The Psychology of the Sopranos: Love, Death, Desire and Betrayal in America's Favorite Gangster Family*, Basic Books, 2002.

Goleman, Daniel, *Emotional Intelligence*, Bloomsbury, 1996.

Gray, John, *Men Are from Mars, Women Are from Venus: A Practical Guide for Improving Communication and Getting What You Want in Your Relationships*, HarperCollins 1992.

Highsmith, Patricia, *The Talented Mr Ripley*, Vintage, 1999.

Hillman, James, *The Soul's Code*, Random House, 1996.

Hobson, Robert, *Forms of Feeling*, Tavistock, 1985.

Kott, Jan, *Shakespeare Our Contemporary*, Methuen, 1965.

Lawrence, D.H., *Apocalypse*, Penguin, 1971.

— *Women in Love*, Penguin, 1971.

Mollon, Phil, *The Fragile Self*, Whurr Publications, 1993.

Olivier, Christiane, trans. G. Craig, *Jocasta's Children*, Routledge, 1989.

Olson, Susan, 'The Shadow', Jung Society of Atlanta, 1999.

O'Neill Dean, Richard, 'Falling in (to the need for) Love', *NZAP Forum Magazine*, 1998.

Rogers, Carl, *On Becoming a Person*, Constable, 1974.

Rowe, Crayton and MacIsaac, David, *Empathic Attunement*, Jason Aronson, 1995.

Steinem, Gloria, *Marilyn: Norma Jeane*, Orion, 1987.

Stevens, Bruce, *Mirror, Mirror*, Psychoz, 2000.

Tannen, Deborah, *That's Not What I Meant!*, HarperCollins, 1990.

Tolkien, J.R.R., *The Lord of the Rings*, various.
Van Sommers, P., *Jealousy*, Pelican, 1986.
Weatherby, W.J., *Conversations with Marilyn*, Sphere, 1977.
Wilson, Andrew, *Beautiful Shadow: A Life of Patricia Highsmith*, Bloomsbury, 2003.
Wilson Knight, G., *The Wheel of Fire*, University Paperbacks, 1961.

Websites
Birchmore, Terry, on-line paper 'Shame and Group Psychotherapy', at
    http://birchmore.org/index.html
Hyman, Edward, on-line interview 'Little Killers', at
    http://www.pbs.org/wgbh/pages/frontline
Vaknin, Sam, 'The Dual Role of the False Self', at http://samvak.tripod.com
Vaknin, Sam, *Malignant Self-Love: Narcissism Revisited*, at
    http://malignantselflove.tripod.com.

Plays
Shaffer, Peter, *Equus*.
Shakespeare, William, *Hamlet*, *King Lear*, *Othello*.

Poems
Coleridge, Samuel Taylor, 'Kubla Khan', 'The Rime of the Ancient Mariner'.
Collins, Billy, 'Victoria's Secret'.
Dickinson, Emily, 'The Heart Asks Pleasure'.

Songs
Dr Hook, 'When You're in Love with a Beautiful Woman'.
Carole King, 'You've Got a Friend'.
Tom Lehrer, 'Oedipus'.
Julie Matthews, 'The Thorn upon the Rose'.
Paul Simon & Art Garfunkel, 'Bridge over Troubled Water'.

Television series
The Sopranos
Nip/Tuck

Films
2001 – A Space Odyssey
Minority Report
Snow White – A Tale of Terror
Shrek
Kill Bill, Volume 1 and *Volume 2*